METROPOLITAN SCHOOL DESEGREGATION

A CASE STUDY OF THE SAINT LOUIS AREA
VOLUNTARY TRANSFER PROGRAM

Michael K. Grady and Charles V. Willie

Graduate School of Education

Harvard University

Wyndham Hall Press

METROPOLITAN SCHOOL DESEGREGATION
A CASE STUDY OF THE SAINT LOUIS AREA VOLUNTARY TRANSFER PROGRAM

Michael K. Grady and Charles V. Willie

Graduate School of Education

Harvard University

Library of Congress Catalog Card Number
86-050425

ISBN 0-932269-88-5

TABLE OF CONTENTS

ACKNOWLEDGMENTS

We gratefully acknowledge the thoughtful and effective way our six staff consultants gathered data on the first year of the voluntary interdistrict transfer program. Joyce Gang, Bridgette Jenkins, Ciby Kimbrough, Mark McMahon, Faith Sandler, and Council Smith conducted the focus groups and telephone interviews and faithfully recorded the opinions of participants. They are to be commended for the professional manner in which they carried out their responsibilities. Special recognition in this regard is given to Faith Sandler, who served as a consultant for the complete term of the project. She organized and assisted with the community group sessions and participated in the editing of the final report.

Also we wish to thank the Voluntary Interdistrict Coordinating Council, its Executive Director, Dr. Susan Uchitelle; and its Director of Data Management, Mr. Michael Erbschloe. The Council provided us with advice on designing and implementing the planning and assessment project. In addition, they gave us access to a substantial data base, the accuracy of which greatly simplified the process by which focus groups were assembled.

We appreciate the support of the Voluntary Interdistrict Coordinating Committee, Dr. Charles McKenna and Dr. James DeClue, its former and current Chairpersons, respectively. Further, the cooperation of every participating school district allowed us to maintain a sense of balance in the various perspectives represented. Special thanks goes to the Division of Evaluation of the Saint Louis Public Schools, which helped us develop samples for magnet school students, parents, and teachers.

The Danforth Foundation provided generous support through a grant to The Graduate School of Education, Harvard University, with which we are affiliated. Dr. Gene Schwilk and Dr. John Ervin recognized the value this project might have for public education and guided our proposal through its preliminary stages.

We also wish to thank Betty Blake, the project secretary, of the Harvard Graduate School of Education, and Mary Christine Grady, who prepared the manuscript for final printing. Katharine O. Parker provided excellent editorial consultation in the preparation of the final manuscript.

Finally, we would like to recognize the more than six hundred adults and students who gave candid and detailed accounts of their experience with the transfer program. In effect, they are the most important contributors to this work and it is our hope that, for their efforts, educational opportunities will be enriched for all students of metropolitan St. Louis and elsewhere.

CHAPTER ONE

INTRODUCTION

According to the Settlement Agreement, the Voluntary Interdistrict Coordinating Council may provide for "collection of data for evaluation of (the) implementation process and identification of problem areas to be targeted for special intervention or additional resources" (VICC, POLICIES, PROCEDURES, AND GUIDELINES, Dec. 1983, p. IX-6).

To implement this responsibility, the Executive Director of the VICC established a relationship with the Harvard Graduate School of Education to determine its interest in an Assessment and Planning Project of the first-year experience of the Voluntary Interdistrict Transfer Program. A happy coincidence of interests was manifested by Harvard University through its Professor of Education and Urban Studies, Dr. Charles V. Willie; Michael Grady, a Saint Louis resident, Washington University graduate, and candidate for the doctoral degree at Harvard; and the Danforth Foundation.

The Danforth Foundation was interested in a project that tapped the perspectives of participants in the program including students, parents, teachers, and other school personnel. Moreover, the Foundation expressed the hope that such information could be made available in a way that would assist in planning for the future. A project was designed by the Harvard representatives to achieve these goals.

Supported by a grant from the Danforth Foundation to Harvard University, the Assessment and Planning Project was established as an independent operation, not under the jurisdiction of VICC, as a way of fostering objectivity in the analysis. It was established, however, according to the VICC guidelines governing research on the Voluntary Interdistrict Transfer Program. The guidelines require approval of the purpose and objective of the research by VICC; this approval was obtained May 2, 1984.

This Assessment and Planning Project presents an analysis of the perceptions of a random sample of both students and their parents and teachers who participated in the implementation of the first year of the Settlement Agreement. According to the Annual Report of the Voluntary Interdistrict Coordinating Council, 2,496 transfer students attended county schools, of whom 2,204 (or 88 percent) were city residents (the others being residents of predominantly black suburban districts) and 351 county residents attended city schools.

A total of 2,847 students participated in the interdistrict transfer program; 77 percent of the participants were city students who transferred to suburban schools and 12 percent were county students who transferred to the city; the remainder (11 percent) were county students who transferred to other county schools.

The number of city and county students who applied to the program was 4,489, a figure slightly one-third greater than the actual participants. All applicants could not be accommodated the first year of implementation for a number of reasons, the principal one being a United States Court of Appeals order September 30, 1983, that "stayed the recruitment process and further transfer of students from the city to the county, pending a hearing before that court" (VICC, ANNUAL REPORT, July 3/5, 1984, pp. 1-3).

This analysis is limited largely to the perceptions of a sample of county white students who attended special programs and magnet schools in the St. Louis Public Schools and to a sample of City of St. Louis black students who attended suburban schools in sixteen districts of the county during the 1983-84 school year. The suburban districts that received racial minority students were Affton, Bayless, Brentwood, Clayton, Hancock Place, Hazelwood, Kirkwood, Ladue, Lindbergh, Mehlville, Parkway, Pattonville, Ritenour, Rockwood, Valley Park, and Webster Groves. The analysis includes the perceptions of a sample of the parents, students, and their teachers. Thus, this report presents information on persons who participated directly and indirectly in the Voluntary Interdistrict Transfer Program. One example of this "indirect participation" is our treatment of community perception of the transfer program presented in Chapter V.

This report omits data on perceptions of city students in regular schools of the St. Louis Public Schools that did not receive county transfer students and the perceptions of their parents. However, it includes data on the perceptions of county residents in areas that did not receive city black students. Data are presented also on suburban black residents, some of whom matriculate in county schools that received city blacks. This report does not include data on city black students in all-black schools or of suburban white students in all-white schools. These populations require more extensive study than time permitted in this project.

The Annual Report of the Voluntary Interdistrict Coordinating Council presents these findings as characteristic of the transfer students the first year of implementation of the program: 93 percent experienced no major disciplinary problem; 90 percent were promoted to the next grade level; 88 percent had regular attendance; and 59 percent were involved in extracurricular activities (VICC ANNUAL REPORT, July 31, 1984, p. iii). This report indicates the feelings of students, teachers, and parents about the first year of implementation and what they believe should be done to improve educational circumstances.

1.1   HISTORY OF THE VOLUNTARY INTERDISTRICT SETTLEMENT PLAN

1.1.1 The Intradistrict Order

In 1972 class action was filed in the U.S. District Court, Eastern District of Missouri, by plaintiffs representing the black parents and school children of St. Louis against the St Louis Board of Education. They were seeking redress for the Board's alleged illegal practice of supporting and maintaining a racially dual school system. Later, the State of Missouri was accused of similar wrongdoing and joined as a party defendant in the case.

Following a protracted but unsuccessful attempt to settle the matter out of court, a trial on the merits was held in 1979. The District Court ruled in favor of the defendants School Board and State of Missouri, finding that the plaintiffs failed to carry the burden of proving that the neighborhood school policy of student assignment was either designed or administered with the intent of maintaining one-race schools (469 F. Supp. 1304).

Early the following year the Eighth Circuit Court of Appeals reversed this decision, ruling that both the Board and the State were liable for the segregated condition of the Saint Louis schools. Further, failure by both parties to take affirmative action to eradicate these vestiges of pre-Brown segregation rendered them both as primary constitutional violators (620 F.2d, 1277).

3

On remand the lower court ordered a comprehensive mandatory reassignment plan for the city system (491 F. Supp. 351). The State of Missouri and the Saint Louis School Board were ordered to divide the costs of this plan. In this same order, issued in 1980, the Court instructed that a good-faith effort be initiated toward the design and implementation of a voluntary interdistrict transfer plan involving the city system and predominantly white Saint Louis suburban school districts. The Court of Appeals affirmed the intradistrict plan and reinforced the lower court's proposal of a metropolitan transfer option (667 F.2d, 643).

The State of Missouri petitioned the U.S. Supreme Court for certiorari. Its principal argument was founded on the premise that it was not responsible for the segregated condition of the Saint Louis schools. Specific to the voluntary interdistrict proposal, it invoked the MILLIKEN rule, asserting that such an interdistrict remedy is inappropriate absent a finding of interdistrict violation. Missouri argued that no such findings of fact had yet been established in the Saint Louis case. The Supreme Court denied certiorari later the same year (454 US 1091).

1.1.2. Negotiating the Voluntary Settlement

The proposal for a voluntary settlement among the Board of Education, a number of the suburban systems and the black plaintiffs was approved by the District Court in July, 1981 (81-2022 Pet.App A73-108). Known as the 12-A Plan, this agreement provided financial incentives for school districts participating in the plan. The Court supported this action by citing precedent which allows for efforts to desegregate a city school system to cross local political boundaries (HILLS V. GAUTREAUX, 425 US 284). The Justice Department submitted an amicus brief in support of the District Court findings. It argued that the racial imbalance of the Saint Louis Public Schools necessitated the involvement of the predominantly white suburbs to effectively desegregate the city system.

Unsatisfied with the progress of the 12-A Plan, black plaintiffs in 1983 moved to join all 23 suburban districts and the State of Missouri in an effort to gain a court-ordered metropolitan remedy. In their petition they argued that the State and all the suburban districts had, with segregative intent, established and maintained dual school systems. Plaintiffs prepared to use evidence of discrimination in housing and land use policy, in combination with a battery of unlawful school policy decisions relevant to district consolidation orders, hiring and retention practices, pupil transportation, student assign-

4

ment, attendance zone gerrymandering, and school construction site selection, among others. The Court approved the motions, set a date for trial, and released its own design for a metropolitan school district consolidation.

Later the same year and one day before the date set for trial, officials from all 23 suburban districts, the Saint Louis Board of Education, and counsel representing black parents and students agreed to support a voluntary interdistrict transfer plan involving all predominantly white suburban districts, thus avoiding a lengthy and complex series of legal proceedings. Parties to the settlement asserted that the plan was dependent on funding from both the State of Missouri and the Saint Louis School Board and petitioned the Court for such an order.

1.1.3. Provisions of the Settlement Plan

The settlement plan for voluntary interdistrict desegregation consists of three basic elements: the voluntary interdistrict transfer program, the quality of education package, and a plan for capital maintenance improvements.

The interdistrict transfer component is a five-year plan for school desegregation, involving the voluntary movement of students into districts and from schools where they are a minority. To date, the largest part of the interdistrict effort has been the transfer of black city students to predominantly white suburban districts. A smaller number of white county students have transferred to the city magnet schools. Presently, the city-to-county transfers outnumber the county-to-city at a rate of approximately nine to one, though officials project this gap will shrink to five to one by 1989.

The settlement also has a multimillion dollar quality of education provision. This is intended to revive the city schools, enabling them to maintain their Missouri AAA rating and to begin approaching the level of opportunity offered by other local school districts. Such factors as reduced class size, restoration of remedial, ancillary, and extracurricular programs; and important part-time integrative programs for children in all-black North Saint Louis schools are part of this proposal.

Finally, a capital improvement package is included to restore the severely deteriorated physical condition of the regular city schools. Funds for this part of the settlement are intended to address the long record of deferred maintenance of the city schools due to a lack of local funding to complete the projects.

The District Court approved the settlement plan and ordered the State of Missouri and the Saint Louis Board of Education to pay for it (83-1721 Pet.App 95a, 108a-119a). The State is obligated to pay for 100 percent of the interdistrict transfer program, plus all quality of education provisions that involved cross-district cooperation. The State and the Board were ordered to share all remaining quality of education components and the capital improvement plan.

In February 1984 the Court of Appeals affirmed the lower court decision with minor modification. Sitting **en banc,** it agreed that the voluntary interdistrict remedy is justified to help correct an intradistrict violation. Further, the involvement of the suburban systems is the only practicable means of effecting any meaningful desegregation of the Saint Louis schools, given the present 80 percent black and brown population, and 20 percent white racial composition of the city system. However, it rescinded from the agreement the State's obligation to pay for any county-to-county transfers of students from predominantly black to predominantly white suburban systems. It ruled that this had no discernible impact on the original intent of the agreement, i.e., the desegregation of the Saint Louis Public Schools.

In its appeal to the U.S. Supreme Court from the Eighth Circuit's decision, the State of Missouri argued that no trial on the merits had established the State's liability for an interdistrict violation. Further, the State argued that it was not signatory to the settlement agreement and should not be obligated to pay for it. The Justice Department and Attorneys General of twenty-four states submitted amicus briefs on the side of the State, supporting its objection to the funding provisions of the settlement plan. On October 1, 1984 the U.S. Supreme Court denied all appeals for certiorari, thereby allowing the continued implementation of the desegregation plan.

1.1.4. Transportation Issues

At the conclusion of the focus group series in the summer of 1984, it was apparent that transportation was the most persistent threat to the viability of the interdistrict transfer program. In light of the vital role played by the Transportation Office, the Supervisor for Desegregation Transportation was consulted for the purpose of clarifying the complexities of the interdistrict transportation scheme. He reported that the most significant characteristic of the interdistrict transportation system, and that which distingusihed it from intradistrict schemes, was the need for individualized attention for each transfer student. The number of variables created by the

6

open enrollment policy of the transfer program created a large margin for error. As a result, students were incorrectly assigned to routes, buses ran off schedule, parents misread schedules, and students spent an inordinately long time in transit.

The large influx of students added to the transfer rolls just days prior to the opening of school in September 1983 was another problem. At that time the Transportation Office did not have the capacity to support such a demand and, as a result, students were not added to transportation routes until the second or third week of classes. With such a sizeable increase in city-to-county transfers the Office was forced to constantly change the structure of the routes and location of bus stops. This became an added burden to an already fragile transportation system.

The Supervisor of Transportation voiced confidence in the drivers' ability to maintain order and safety standards on the school buses. Nonetheless, he shifted the responsibility onto the shoulders of school building principals. He noted the high degree of successful transportation experiences with students from schools with principals who communicate with their drivers and take drivers' reports of student misconduct seriously.

The Supervisor has signed contracts with three bus companies for transportation-related services for 1984-85. One bus company provided most of the vehicles for last year's transportation. The Supervisor projects that a heightened sense of competition among the three will result in a more reliable and higher quality service.

The Supervisor reported that fewer than one-third the number of taxi cabs used in 1983-84 will be part of the regular transportation system in 1984-85. He cautioned, however, that cabs will never be completely eliminated from the plan due to their cost-effectiveness in transporting some students.

The Supervisor voiced concern over the insufficient operating budget appropriated for the Transportation Office. Though transportation-related expenditures are part of the court order, Transportation Office operating expenses must be appropriated by the state legislature. The defiant posture many state legislators have taken toward school desegregation has all but frozen the desegregation budget at an insufficient level.

At the request of the Missouri Department of Elementary and Second-

7

ary Education, and in response to a recommendation issued in our first report, Ecotran Systems, Inc. conducted a study of the transportation system for the voluntary interdistrict transfer program during the fall of 1984. The research team concluded that three major policy areas required revision to improve the effectiveness of the current transportation scheme. The areas targeted for attention are communication, policy and procedures, and data management.

The Ecotran representatives observed that the experience of the first eighteen months of implementation had created an adversarial relationship between the State of Missouri and the participating districts (as represented by the VICC). It noted the importance of reopening channels of communication and to this end recommended that meetings involving all interests be conducted on a regular basis. It also recommended the appointment of a representative of the court to mediate policy disputes which arise periodically. This would allow the parties an alternative to the district court for the resolution of disputed policy decisions by the transportation office.

The Ecotran team members also reviewed the policies and procedures of the VICC and the Desegregation Transportation Office and recommended modifying two current practices. First, it advised substituting a "deadline concept" for the current practice of "first come-first serve" processing of applications for interdistrict transfers. Ecotran consultants felt this would improve the administrative efficiency of the process in addition to promoting equity and fairness in the assignment of students to districts. The second practice and policy issue addressed by the study was orientation for students and their parents. Currently suburban districts require a visitation by all families who have applied for interdistrict transfer. Ecotran recognized the importance of this practice but advised that it occur only after acceptance of the student by the district. This would dispel the notion held by some that districts are screening candidates on the basis of a personal interview. Ecotran also had a second transportation-related recommendation, that the "zoning concept" for student assignments mentioned in our first report (for the purpose of attaining greater efficiency) should not be implemented, that greater efficiency in student assignments could be accomplished without restricting a student's choice to a specific cluster of schools.

Finally, Ecotran recommended that the current computerized routing system be replaced by one with a greater capacity to withstand the constant demand for routing modifications. Also, the report advised that the VICC-maintained student data base be shared with

the state transportation office. The report concluded that the introduction of appropriate transportation-related technology would
"improve the responsiveness, stability, and efficiency" of the system.

The Ecotran Systems, Inc. report was entitled "St. Louis City and
Metropolitan Area Voluntary Interdistrict Transfer Program Transpor-
tation Analysis Final Report". It was authored by David A. Bennett,
Superintendent of Saint Paul, Minnesota Public Schools (former
Deputy Superintendent of Milwaukee Public Schools), John R. Thome,
David J. Blozy, and Kurt Grigsby, and was submitted November
1984, two months after preparation of our first report that indicated
serious transportation problems.

1.2. DATA AND METHOD

1.2.1. Purpose of the Project

This report provides a descriptive record of the perceptions of a
sample of students, parents, and teachers who were directly and
indirectly involved in the Saint Louis voluntary interdistrict desegregation plan in 1983-84. The patterns of interaction described are without
verification by alternative data. They represent the frequently
stated observations and opinions of those individuals who agreed
to participate in focus groups or telephone interviews. The use
of perceptions, opinions, and attitudes as the chief source of data
is a limitation of this study that should be considered in the interpreta-
tion of findings.

Essentially, this is a policy study. Our hope is that this report will
provide a useful planning tool for local educational policy makers,
when linked with other information. Several years of implementation
remain in the interdistrict transfer program and an assessment of
first-year effects such as this should help educators and policy makers
sharpen their plans for subsequent stages of the program. It should
also provide a source of information for local parents, teachers,
business and government leaders, and community groups interested
in quality education for all students of the Saint Louis metropolitan
area.

1.2.2. Method

The foundation of the planning and assessment project was use of
the focus group to elicit and record the perceptions of individuals
directly and indirectly involved in the transfer program. Thirty
of these groups consisting of 147 panelists met over the course of

the summer of 1984. During the fall of 1984, 26 community representatives were assembled in 7 additional focus groups. Each group
of four to seven was classified according to the specific type of
experience that participants had with the interdistrict desegregation
program.

Individuals in the suburban areas were randomly selected from lists
of students, parents, and school personnel nominated by the chief
school officer or his representative, as persons knowledgeable of
the schools and the interdistrict transfer program. Individuals were
contacted by letter from Harvard headquarters, requesting their
voluntary participation in the project. Written communication was
followed up by telephone contact from the group leaders in Saint
Louis. Group sessions were held at convenient locations in the city
and county. Participants other than community representatives
were offered $15.00 as reimbursement for transportation and other
expenses associated with participating in a group meeting. City
students were randomly selected from applicants to the Voluntary
Interdistrict Transfer Program. They too were contacted as described
above.

Groups met in sessions that ranged from ninety minutes to two and
one-half hours. Discussions were conducted by trained professionals
with prior experience in education and other human service fields,
and were tape-recorded. Group leaders generated discussion around
a specified topic, focusing on a predetermined set of issues relevant
to the participants' personal involvement with the transfer program.
Within two days of the meeting the group leader and observer submitted summary memos of the discussion.

In this report we discuss findings relevant to the seven types of
direct or indirect experience with the transfer program. Data are
presented also from the vantage point of community observers.
This report does not include data on students and teachers in regular
Saint Louis public schools, i.e., those that are not classified as magnets.

The report is organized into chapters that describe the experience
of black students and parents, white students and parents, and professional educators from the city and suburban districts; and the observations of representatives of community groups. We have divided
the city experience into categories corresponding to our focus-group
organization: city black residents currently enrolled in a suburban
district, those who enrolled and withdrew from a suburban school,
city black students who applied for transfer in 1983 but who had

10

not been accommodated in a suburban school during the 1983-84 school year. The chapter on white residents is comprised of the perspectives of county-to-city white magnet-transfer students who have withdrawn from the program and returned to their home suburban districts, white suburban students who never transferred to the city but remained in suburban schools, and city white students who volunteered to attend city magnet schools. In another chapter we report on the observations of city magnet teachers, suburban district personnel, participating school district superintendents, and the Supervisor of the Desegregation Transportation Office. Finally, we have a chapter on the observations of local community group leaders.

It became apparent after the first week of focus-group meetings that an important element of the population was being neglected by our original design. We found that many individuals contacted were interested in sharing their reactions to the transfer program, but were unable or unwilling to participate in a group discussion. Telephone interviews were arranged to accommodate such persons. The research staff that led focus groups contacted approximately 350 parents and students. We sampled heaviest in those categories of greatest import and in those which had a disproportionately small yield in the focus-group phase of the project. Phone interview questions were similar to those asked of individuals who participated in focus group discussions. Mid-November marked the completion of all data collection, resulting in the documentation of the perceptions of approximately 600 respondents.

1.2.3. Data

This report is based on an analysis of data drawn from the summary memos prepared by group leaders and observers, transcripts of focus-group sessions, telephone interviews recorded on schedules, field notes of the project leaders who personally interviewed chief school officers or their representatives, newspaper articles, and documents of the Voluntary Interdistrict Coordinating Council. Participants in focus groups and telephone interviews were quoted verbatim when possible. Comments from these reports are given in the section of each chapter called "Case Illustrations." The quotes represent some of the raw data on which the report is based.

1.2.4. Research Staff

Six adult members of the Saint Louis community were hired in June 1984 to serve as group leaders in the planning and assessment project. These individuals had previous training and experience in conducting group discussions. As residents of Saint Louis, they were also familiar with the details of the voluntary interdistrict settlement plan.

The racially balanced staff was composed of two males and four females. Three of the consultants were in the final stage of completing doctoral work in counseling and clinical psychology. Another had recently defended a master's thesis in cultural anthropology. The fifth is a practicing attorney, and the sixth has two graduate degrees -- a master's in social work and a doctoral degree in educational policy and administration.

The staff met for three training sessions prior to the first focus-group meeting. These sessions included simulation work as participant observers. Also, they gave the group an opportunity to share individual styles and approaches developed in previous projects. Prominent attention was given to the details of the settlement plan, particularly the mechanical procedures relevant to student application and transfer. Dr. Susan Uchitelle, Executive Director of the Voluntary Interdistrict Coordinating Council, participated in a training session to share her expertise and to answer questions concerning the obligations of the suburban districts and the role of the Coordinating Committee and Council in the administration of the settlement. Finally, the group met at the end of the first week of focus-group discussions for the purpose of reviewing the strengths and weaknesses of the research design and any personal difficulties experienced during the first sessions. The field director of the project participated in most of the focus-group discussions. His presence was an additional quality control activity.

1.3. STATISTICAL PROFILE OF SAMPLE GROUPS

This study of the opinions and attitudes of students and parents in city and suburban settings is designed to reveal the experiential themes common among individuals who have participated in similar desegregation events. While similar social experiences tend to beget similar individual responses, adaptation in social relations also is a function of personal characteristics. Analyzed here are variations in the personal characteristics of the black and the white persons who participated in this study. Included are samples of city and suburban students who attended city magnet schools, samples of city students who transferred to suburban schools, and samples of county residents who attended suburban schools. This analysis represents students who enrolled and remained in school the full term. Those who withdrew from the program are omitted from the statistical part of this analysis.

The sample of students in our study who participated in the city magnet school program consisted of 12 city blacks, 10 city whites, and 36 suburban or county whites. Because of the small numbers in the various categories, these findings should be accepted with caution as descriptive but not definitive results.

Table 1.1

Characteristics of Participants Enrolled
in City Magnet Schools, Saint Louis, 1984:

Race and Residence of Magnet-School Samples

Student Characteristics	N=12 City Blacks	N=10 City Whites	N=36 County Whites
Age of parents (average years)	42	39	42
Children per household (average)	2.7	4.0	2.4
Family Composition (%)			
Female head of household	67	20	29
Other	33	80	71
Occupation (%)			
Professional, executive, managerial	17	10	13
Semi-professional	8	40	28
Skilled	42	20	41
Unskilled	25	30	14
Unemployed	8	--	4
Grade Level (%)			
Elementary	25	40	25
Middle	25	40	28
Secondary	50	20	47

There are city magnet schools at all levels, and we included students in all levels in our samples. As seen in Table 1.1, a majority of black students and of white students in the combined samples were in middle or secondary school; some were in elementary schools too. The black city residents in our sample who attended city magnet schools were different from the white city residents in our sample. On the average, the magnet school, white, city residents at 39 years were 3 years younger than the magnet-school, black, city residents in our sample; they averaged 4 children per family which was about 1 child more than the average number of children per family among city blacks in the magnet school sample.

The whites and the blacks in the magnet-school samples also were different in family composition and in occupation of parents. A majority of the whites in the sample were members of two-parent households compared with a majority of blacks who were members of single-parent households. Whites in the magnet-school sample were about equally divided between white-collar and blue-collar jobs. In summary, city whites in the magnet school sample were younger and had larger families and higher status jobs than did blacks in this sample.

The city whites in the magnet school sample also were younger and had larger families than suburban whites in the sample who transferred their children to city magnet schools. However, occupation and family composition were similar for these groups of the same race. They were about equally distributed in blue-collar and in white-collar work and a majority of suburban whites in city magnet schools as well as city whites in these schools were members of two-parent families.

As seen in Table 1.2, the county whites in the sample whose children remained in suburban schools were quite different from the sample of county whites whose children transferred to city magnet schools. While family size was similarly small (less than three children per household) in these two samples of suburban whites and parents of those who remained in suburban schools, in age they averaged only 3 years or more than parents of county-to-city, magnet school transfers. White parents in suburban communities in our sample whose children continued to attend schools were substantially different in occupation and in family status. Nearly all of the sample of suburban white families whose offspring attended schools outside the city were members of two-parent households, and four-fifths of the parents in these families pursued white-collar work, the highest

14

proportion in executive, professional, and managerial occupations. In summary, suburban whites in our sample who elected to remain in suburban schools tended to have relatively older parents and lived in predominantly two-parent households. A majority of the parents worked in high-prestige white-collar jobs, compared to the parents of suburban whites in our sample who transferred their offspring to city magnet schools.

Table 1.2

Characteristics of Participants Enrolled in County Schools, Saint Louis, 1984:

Race and Residence of County-School Samples

Student Characteristics	N=183 City Blacks	N=22 County Blacks	N=26 County Whites
Age of parents (average years)	40	46	45
Children per household (average)	2.5	2.5	2.7
Family Composition (%)			
Female head	43	33	5
Other	57	67	95
Occupation (%)			
Professional, executive managerial	2	11	39
Semi-professional	21	45	33
Skilled	19	22	28
Unskilled	42	22	--
Unemployed	16	--	--
Grade Level (%)			
Elementary	36	14	15
Middle	25	14	12
Secondary	39	72	73

City blacks who transferred to suburban schools are in families whose parents are about 2 years younger than those who remained in city magnet schools, according to Table 1.2. However, they had similarly small families of less than 3 children per household. Their occupation are similar, too, in that a majority of the parents of city blacks in city magnet schools and those who transferred to suburban schools are blue-collar workers. A difference between the samples of these two groups in the black population is family composition: a majority of city blacks whose children transferred to suburban schools are in two-parent households compared with a minority of those enrolled in city magnet schools, as seen in Tables 1.1 and 1.2. Thus, city blacks, in our sample, who sought education in suburban schools rather than in city magnet schools tended to have relatively younger parents, a majority of whom lived as husband and wife in two-parent households. In this respect, they differed from the city parents of blacks who sought quality education for their children in city magnet schools. The two groups of blacks were similar, however, in occupational characteristics of parents; both groups were disproportionately employed in blue-collar jobs.

As indicated in Table 1.2, blacks who are residents of the city but who send their children to suburban schools are much younger than resident blacks in these school systems. The average black parent who lives in the suburbs tends to be relatively older than the average parent in the city. Suburban blacks also tend to have the highest rate of family stability, compared with city samples of blacks. Finally, black suburban residents tend to hold a higher proportion of white-collar jobs than blacks in any of the other samples. The major similarity between suburban blacks and city blacks is their family size: all are relatively small, averaging 2.5 to 2.7 children per household.

In family size, family composition, and employment status, suburban blacks are more similar to some suburban whites who elect to send their children to city magnet schools than to samples of their own racial group who live in the city. A difference between black and white similar populations is the relatively older age level of parents in the black suburban families. They average 4 years more than some of their suburban white neighbors, especially those who volunteered to send their children to city magnet schools.

As mentioned earlier, the data in Tables 1.1 and 1.2 were not presented for the purpose of generalizing the results to all blacks and all whites in the city and county populations. Since interviewees and participants in focus groups were randomly selected, however, they

16

do manifest in general ways some of the characteristics of others similarly situated. With caution and based on this analysis, we offer these tentative patterns about the kinds of families who experienced various kinds of involvements in the interdistrict school desegregation program.

Among the tentative conclusions about blacks, we offer these. Blacks in city and suburban sectors of the same metropolitan area are not a monolithic population. City black families with children in public schools tend to be younger than suburban black families with children in public schools, and city black families tend to be less stable in parental composition than are their suburban racial counterparts. Also, the suburban black families tend to have a higher proportion of white-collar jobs than do the city blacks. Despite the age disparity of parents in these two groups of the same racial population, city and suburban blacks whose children are enrolled in the city magnet schools or suburban schools have similarly small households.

Among tentative conclusions about whites, we make these statements. Whites in city and in suburban sectors of the same metropolitan area are not a monolithic population. City white families with children in public schools tend to be younger than suburban white families with children in public schools. White families who choose to remain in their home suburban districts tend to be better off economically and older than other whites in the suburbs who volunteer to send their children to city magnet schools, or city whites with children in such schools. These latter two white populations are similar in socioeconomic status, although the parents in city white families tend to be younger and larger than their suburban white counterparts whose children also attend city magnet schools. A majority of white families in city and in suburban settings tend to be two-parent units; but suburban white families who send their children to suburban schools tend to have the highest proportion of two-parent families.

Across racial lines, suburban black residents differ socioeconomically in a substantial way from city blacks whose children attend city magnet schools, as well as from city blacks who transfer their children to the suburbs. In this respect, the suburban blacks are more similar to suburban whites who elect to bus their children to the city for an education. Also across racial lines, city whites who send their children to city magnet schools are more similar socioeconomically to suburban blacks than they are to suburban whites whose children remain in suburban schools.

17

There are many similarities between city whites who seek a quality education for their offspring in the city and suburban blacks who seek a quality education for their children in the suburbs; there are several differences between city black families with children enrolled in city magnet or suburban schools and suburban blacks who are residents of suburban areas. And there are many differences between suburban white families who elect to send their children to local suburban school systems and other whites, both in the city and the suburbs, who volunteer to enroll their children in city magnet schools.

While the search for a quality education was a common experience for all five groups described in this study (city blacks in magnet schools, city blacks in suburban schools, suburban blacks in suburban schools, suburban whites in suburban schools, and suburban whites in city magnet schools) the most radical differences between one group and all others were: (1) the younger age of parents in city white families and their relative larger family size compared to all others; (2) the older age of parents in suburban black families compared to all others; (3) the higher proportion of single-parent households among city blacks with children in magnet schools compared to all others; (4) the higher socioeconomic status and family stability of suburban whites with children in suburban schools compared to all others. Similarities among some of these groups across racial lines had to do with age of parents, family stability, size of household, and socioeconomic status. Thus, geographic location, socioeconomic status, age, and race are situational variables that may condition individual responses, and that should be considered when attempting to understand the adaptation of families to schools and educational opportunities. A knowledge of race and socioeconomic status is important, but knowledge of these characteristics alone is insufficient for gaining a full understanding of adaptation. Other factors and features discussed in this analysis must be considered.

REFERENCES

Bennett, David A., John R. Thome, David J. Plozy, and Kurt Grigsby. "St. Louis city and Metropolitan Area Voluntary Interdistrict Transfer Program Transportation Analysis Final Report." Cleveland: Ecotran Systems, Inc., November 1984.

U.S. District Court, Eastern District of Missouri
   469 F. Supp. 1304
   491 F. Supp. 351
   81-2022 Pet.-App A73-108
   83-1721 Pet.App 95A, 108a-119a

U.S. Eighth Circuit Court of Appeals
   620 F.2d, 1277
   667 F.2d, 643

U.S. Supreme Court
   425 US 284, HILLS V. GAUTREAUX
   454 US 1091

Voluntary Interdistrict Coordinating Council
   ANNUAL REPORT, July 31, 1984
   POLICIES, PROCEDURES, AND GUIDELINES, December 1983

CHAPTER TWO

PERCEPTIONS OF BLACK STUDENTS AND PARENTS

The following chapter is an account of the perceptions of city black parents and students who are presently or were at one time involved in the voluntary interdistrict transfer program. The first section of the chapter relates the observations of students and parents of students currently transferring from the Saint Louis Public Schools to a suburban Saint Louis County school district. The second section is a discussion of parent and student perceptions of city blacks who were enrolled in the city-to-county transfer program but who have since withdrawn. Another section represents the views of parents and students who had applied to interdistrict transfer in 1983 but who were not allowed to change districts due to a stay issued by the court shortly after the start of school. The final two sections are of city blacks connected with city magnet schools and of suburban blacks connected with suburban school systems. Like all sections of this report, these are composed of discussions of what participants felt were the most compelling issues related to their transfer experience.

2.1. CITY BLACK STUDENTS WHO TRANSFERRED TO AND REMAINED IN SUBURBAN SCHOOLS

This section describes the experiences of city black students and parents who transferred from the city system to a suburban school district. These observations are principally those of the first-year transfers; a separate discussion of city black students with multiple-year experience in suburban systems is presented at the conclusion of the section. This focus group of active transfer students is of value as it portrays an experience that is essentially positive, thus representing the most satisfactory elements of the program.

Six focus groups of active-transfer participants were conducted for this category. Three groups consisting of a total of sixteen parents met to discuss the issues relevant to their children's transfer exper-

20

ience. All parent participants were either mothers, aunts, or grand-
mothers of the students. Three student focus groups were held for
this category, representing grades 4, 9, 11 and 12. Sixteen such
students were involved in these panel discussions.

One hundred and seventy-eight black transfer students or parents
of these students were reached by phone for a discussion that lasted,
on average, fifteen minutes. Parents represented 59 percent of
the respondents and of these, over 90 percent were mothers or other
adult females living in the home.

2.1.1. Discovery of Transfer Program

The opportunity to transfer to the county was brought to the attention
of city black families through a variety of channels. Parents often
discovered the program through news reports in the local media.
Widespread coverage of the desegregation plan and its on-going
litigation has served as a reminder of the transfer opportunity, too.

Word of mouth has also been an effective vehicle of communication.
Students participating in the program have described their experiences
to friends and relatives, and this has contributed to the rising number
of applications for transfer.

Finally, families have discovered the transfer program through official, school-related channels. In some cases this included discussions
with staff from the Saint Louis Public Schools' Recruitment Office;
in others, the information was gleaned from brochures and handouts
distributed by the Voluntary Interdistrict Coordinating Council.

In general, parents and students do not systematically "shop" for
districts in which to enroll. Some based their choice on the public
reputation of the school district and the image that that district
carries throughout the community. Others are satisfied with any
suburban district assigned to them. Parents also report their choice
of districts was influenced by how readily a district responded to
their initial application for transfer. In some cases a district that
had originally been a family's second or third choice would be selected
because it was the first to contact the applicant. Of course, as
the program has expanded another important determinant in the
choice of a district was the presence of siblings, friends, or relatives
already enrolled.

2.1.2. Reasons for Transfer

Parents and students involved in the voluntary interdistrict transfer program in 1983-84 reported that their decision to leave the Saint Louis Public Schools was motivated primarily by an expectation of better educational opportunities in suburban districts. When asked to describe what constitutes a good education, they typically referred to four areas of concern: quality of instruction, condition of school facilities, class size, and student discipline.

Transfer students and their parents were especially sensitive to the issue of teaching. Frequently they would characterize suburban teachers as effective motivators of student achievement and concerned with the children's emotional development.

Parents described suburban teachers, in general, as talented and excellent resources. Many said there was good parent-teacher communication. When problems occurred, teachers often contacted parents by telephone. This fostered further involvement with the school by parents. A few suburban teachers were described as mean and prejudiced against blacks. However, parents said that most of the teachers in suburban schools were helpful.

We also asked Saint Louis students and parents why they withdrew from the city schools. Some had children in parochial schools but preferred public schools and took advantage of the opportunity to enroll in such schools in the county. Others transferred because of dissatisfaction with the Saint Louis Public Schools. These statements of dissatisfaction should be interpreted as perceptions that may or may not have factual basis. Nevertheless, they are included so that the district is aware of the public image it projects. Among the alleged deficiencies of city public schools are their poor condition of physical facilities and equipment, crowded classrooms, limited extracurricular activities especially with reference to sports in elementary schools, inadequate supply of instructional materials, few advanced courses in the natural sciences and computer instruction, and insufficient attention to students with learning difficulties and other special needs.

These deficiencies, parents said, were associated with increased behavior problems in city schools and contributed to low teacher morale. As evidence of the probable validity of these allegations, information was received from some city teachers who had transferred their own children from city to suburban schools and who had advised other parents to do likewise.

22

Again, we emphasize that these are statements of perception. Also, they are perceptions that parents and their offspring have of regular city schools. They do not apply to magnet schools. For some, these perceptions are offered to justify or rationalize a transfer decision.

2.1.3. Apprehensions of City Students Prior to Transfer

Black students were fearful that they would be treated like strangers in their new schools. Some reported they were the object of stares. Their ultimate worry was that they might be rejected by their new classmates. Transfer students were also preoccupied with the possibility of not being academically prepared to compete with resident students of the suburban districts.

The threat of racial prejudice was an ever-present worry of the transfer student. Some parents alerted their children to expect to be put in a position where they would need to make "believers" of a skeptical suburban audience.

Several students encountered unpleasant circumstances that confirmed their apprehension. There were reported cases of name-calling among students. In one school, white students circulated a petition requesting black students to withdraw from "their" school. A parent had to transfer her children from one suburban district to another because a teacher publicly ridiculed her child, who had a learning disability. Some students felt they were ignored by a teacher when they tried to participate in classroom discussions.

Fears of isolation, friendlessness, prejudice, and academic adequacy were abated, in part, in districts that sponsored programs that specifically addressed these concerns. Among such programs were student and parent orientations, "host" families, "buddy systems," faculty workshops on multicultural relations, and friendship clubs. Strong administrative leadership that promoted acceptance of the transfer students was also recognized by parents as contributing to a healthy school climate.

2.1.4. Race Relations and Student Adjustment

In general, students and parents speak highly of the relationship that developed between black and white students in the suburban districts. They credit imaginative strategies of many of the teachers and principals in responding to the new challenges of the integrated classroom. These strategies include candid student discussion of

23

issues related to ethnic diversity, black awareness workshops, the incorporation of key black historical figures in the curriculum, and the expansion of the school library's collection of black authors.

A minor concern of the transfer students is the frustration they experience when resident students "try too hard" to make them feel at home. In some cases, they go so far as to imitate black speech patterns, handshakes, and athletic and musical interests. Transfer students believe that suburban students who "try too hard" are not really sincere.

Other adjustment problems experienced by city transfer students were related to social life and leisure, study habits, and the budgeting of free time. Because of the distance factor, some transfer students found it difficult to participate in after-school activities; many of these same students experienced great difficulty in adjusting to their new school. The increased academic workload left little time for socializing with neighborhood friends. In nearly all cases in which students experienced a positive experience in making new friends, this experience was explained as largely due to their participation in after-school activities.

Several other important features of the process of student socialization were cited by students and parents. First, older students complained that districts did little to further adjustment beyond the school tour and basic orientation. Many experienced anxiety after being given a schedule and left to fend on their own. Second, the nature of student concerns varied greatly depending on the grade level of the student. Older students were reportedly more preoccupied with issues related to interpersonal relations, including racial tensions, and making new friends. Their younger siblings, on the other hand, were more concerned with the mechanical aspects of the transfer: getting up in the morning, catching the bus, getting home safely in the evening, etc.

2.1.5. Persisting Problems

In panel discussions and telephone interviews the most prominent issue raised by both transfer students and their parents was transportation. The discussion often focused on the problems associated with the ride to the suburbs and included the reliability of the new system, the attitude and deportment of the bus drivers, and the incidents of misbehavior on school buses.

Interestingly, students more frequently called attention to the unreliability of the buses and tendency to run off-schedule. The students expressed less concern with the length of the bus ride. They conveyed a willingness to endure a long ride if they could be assured of a reliable schedule. It is when children are left waiting on street corners that problems emerge. Distance, however, is a more pressing concern for parents.

Parents are concerned for the safety of children on the buses. They have called into question the capacity of a bus driver to be both driver and disciplinarian; they feel this is too heavy a burden for one person and, consequently, creates a threat to student safety. They argue that the frequency of misbehavior enroute to school warrants the presence of monitors on interdistrict transfer buses. Parents fear that many of the negative elements they associated with city schools exist on the bus rides to and from the suburban schools. These include alleged drug use, unruly behavior, and bad language.

Academic adjustment was another key concern. Many hours of remedial work were required to bring some students up to grade level. Parents and students alike praised the efforts of teachers who fostered such progress in a short amount of time, through tutorials and individualized instruction.

Parents found themselves more involved in the child's classwork largely due to the increased amount of homework and better communication between teacher and parent about student progress. Students were also forced to budget their time more effectively. The length of time in transit demanded from the students a more disciplined approach to studies, especially if they were involved in extracurricular activities.

2.1.6. Multiyear Transfer Experience

An intriguing perspective was offered by one segment of the population under study, the black parents and students who have been participating in the transfer program for longer than one year. These discussants helped shed light on several of the adjustment difficulties. City students reflected on the initial reluctance of suburban students to accept their presence in the county districts. In general, they discovered that hostility toward them was attenuated over the course of time and lessened further with the addition of more black students to the transfer rolls. This is an important observation in that some

25

administrators are inclined to react to racial tension by decreasing the number of minority students. Where the number of racial minorities was nonexistent or very small in the past, a temporary increase in racial tension may be expected with any increase in the size of the minority population.

Students credited school staff leadership for facilitating their adjustment to their new schools. They indicated that effective intervention by building principals, counselors, classroom teachers, and desegregation coordinators was instrumental in creating what they judged to be a pleasant learning environment.

Parents of the multiyear transfer students hastened to advise that in the process of desegregating their schools, districts should favor younger children, citing their experience that adjustment problems with their preteens were less severe than with older children.

It should be added, individuals in this group with more than one year of desegregation experience were adamant in their belief that suburban school districts are systematically screening applicants in search of the academically most capable students. They referred to the administration of elaborate admissions examinations prior to acceptance. This perception might be explained in part by the fact that admissions examinations were sometimes administered when families first enrolled in the transfer program under the 12-A Plan.

2.1.7. Case Illustrations

This section represents the perceptions of black students and their parents who have transferred from the Saint Louis Public Schools and are currently enrolled in a suburban district.

As a general rule, black families chose to transfer their children to suburban districts for the purpose of receiving "a better education." They perceived county school districts as "more orderly learning environments" with "more extensive curricular offerings" than are available in the city schools.

Several parents discussed the level of sacrifice interdistrict transfer requires, one commenting, "I was so happy to get them in, to get a better education, whatever sacrifice I had to make it didn't mattter." Others related their children's perceptions of the quality of their new schools, saying, "They comment on how much more they've learned." Another parent, recognizing the importance of homework,

26

remarked, "That was a change for them, but (their teacher) warned them, 'you take your books home.'" One parent characterized her comment to quality education by saying, "It does make a big difference in their attitudes and everything; some parents don't want to make the sacrifices. It takes time, you have to take off work. But in the long run, your children are doing better and are happier."

Students expressed some apprehensions attendant to interdistrict transfer such as fears of not being equal to the academic rigor of their new schools, losing ties to their city neighborhood, and being subjected to racial stereotyping in county districts. Students and parents reported that race relations among students were generally quite good and that students who were more active in extracurricular activities socialized quickly and developed a sense of ownership in their new schools. There were more scattered reports of racial tension often during the first months of newly desegregated classroom settings. One mother recounted a conversation she had with a daughter who suspected she was the victim of a prejudiced teacher: "Her teacher refused to help her with a problem. I visited him and brought this to his attention. My daughter said her teacher ridiculed her in front of her classmates, saying 'she doesn't understand me, I guess, because I'm white.'" Another student reported, "This one teacher made it real hard for me to pass her class. She'd grade a paper and it seemed like my answers were like the white girls,' but mine would be wrong and theirs would be right."

Regarding extracurricular activities, one parent of a student suggested that race was a factor in student selection: "My daughter wanted to go out for cheerleading, and she went to this whole tryout bit with three other blacks and they didn't get a part. The girls seemed to think that they didn't get it because they were black. I asked if they tried to qualify, did they meet the standards? And they said 'yes, that's how we got far enough for the tryouts.'"

Finally, transfer families indicated that the most persistent problems resulted from deficiencies in the transportation system. These included late buses, unsupervised trips to and from suburban districts, and long walks through dangerous neighborhoods. In one meeting, several elementary school students shared with us some of the difficulties associated with living far from school. "You have to get up too early in the morning to do that; I just wished I lived closer to school." "I wanna walk to school with my friends." Others in the same group compared their experience to that of their friends and classmates who are residents of the suburban district: "... and

27

they don't have all the hassle of getting to school in the morning."
"There's a boy, he lives right across from school and he gets to ride
his bike to school." A parent noted, "Transportation is a terrible
problem. They have to walk about three long blocks. It's not the
distance that's so bad but the neighborhood they have to go through
to catch the bus; and early in the morning it's dark and I worry for
their safety."

2.2. CITY BLACK STUDENTS WHO TRANSFERRED TO AND WITH-DREW FROM SUBURBAN SCHOOLS

This category of discussants involves black students and parents
who transferred from the city system to a suburban district in 1983-84,
but who subsequently became dissatisfied and withdrew from the
program. They offer a helpful perspective since their experience
highlights the perceived deficiencies of the transfer experience.

Two adult focus groups of three and five parents met to relate the
reasons for their children's return to their original city schools.
Of the eight adults, two males were in attendance. A third group
of three middle-school students represented the student perspective
for this category.

Seventeen parents and three students who had withdrawn from the
program were contacted by telephone. Just fewer than 80 percent
of the adult respondents were females.

2.2.1. Academic Difficulty

Many city parents who chose to withdraw their children from the
transfer program reported that they were unable to adjust to the
academic rigor of their new schools. With such a strong component
of remedial work required to bring some up to grade level, in tandem
with their regular course work, the children were often overwhelmed.
Academically-related withdrawals were frequently reported especially
among students with learning difficulties. They were unable to
cope with the more demanding and competitive classroom environment, despite the special help offered by their teachers. Inability
to keep pace in an accelerated academic program was a source of
frustration that sometimes manifested itself in disruptive behavior.

A few college-bound students were also worried that a lower grade
point average would jeopardize their chances to attend the college
of their choice. In these limited cases students believed a return

28

to the city would improve their college chances, reasoning that higher GPAs in the city would be more impressive than a weaker record from a suburban school district.

2.2.2. Behavior Problems

Behavior problems of students were described by parents as "personality clashes" with teachers, rivalry with students resident in the county, and run-ins sometimes resulting in fights among transfer peers on the bus and with other students in the suburban schools. Clearly some of these disputes were associated with communication breakdowns between students and teachers and between city and suburban students because of the different cultural contexts from which each group emerged.

Suburban schools were said to be more strict in enforcing their codes of conduct. Thus, when serious violations occurred, they were inclined to suspend the students. While preferring the county schools, city students who were suspended or who experienced academic difficulty sometimes returned to city schools to avoid further "hassles."

2.2.3. Race Relations

Racial prejudice on the part of the host district teachers and students figured prominently in transfer students' decisions to return to their city schools. The most common form of racial hostility involved name-calling among students, but rarely did this lead a child to drop from the program. Far more frequently, children complained that teachers did not understand them. They claimed that incidents or remarks by black students were being misconstrued by school staff. This misunderstanding would sometimes lead to a confrontation and, in some cases, suspension.

On a less frequent basis, middle- and high-school students reported more overt forms of racism by teachers: casual references to racial stereotypes, differential treatment for white and for black students, refusal by instructors to call on black students during class discussion, and the like.

Some city black students believed that they were recruited for the purpose of improving the school's athletic program. Such students were required to spend an inordinate amount of time on the practice field, at the expense of valuable study time. They and their parents felt exploited. Other students, however, withdrew from suburban

29

schools because they were not allowed to play on the school team or participate in other after-school activities. Some athletically oriented city students were discouraged when they discovered that the suburban school they chose had fewer varsity athletic opportunities than the city school from which they transferred. As these students saw it, the grass is not always greener on the suburban side of the fence, and this observation was contrary to their expectations. Parents also hesitated to enroll their children in districts where the percentage of black students was still very low. There were reports of transfer students withdrawing in places where they were the only blacks in a classroom. City students who withdrew from suburban school systems report that it was often not one but a combination of factors that pushed them away from suburban schools.

2.2.4. Transportation

A persistent cause of city student withdrawals from suburban schools in 1983-84 was the failure of buses and cabs to maintain their schedules. Parents complained that late morning buses forced their children to miss their first-hour class, in some cases so frequently that they fell substantially behind their classmates. Late return trips in the evening limited the students' leisure and study time.

Some students related that even when transportation ran smoothly, the early morning departure was too much to bear. In some instances children were required to be at their bus stops before sunrise. This, combined with a late evening return and heavy homework assignments, resulted in little time for students to interact with neighborhood friends.

Distance was definitely a key element in some families' decision to withdraw from the program. Teachers reported that children sometimes appeared weary upon completing their morning bus ride. Parents of younger students expressed a sense of insecurity with their children going to school so far from their homes. Parents mentioned fear that they would be helpless if their children were to become sick or injured. Also they worried that the distance factor prevented them from being more active in the district's parent-teacher organizations and their children's school-related activities. They also observed that many parent activities are scheduled during the day, precluding the participation of working mothers and fathers. The children, too, were concerned about the length of the bus ride; but their concern had to do more with the unreliability of the bus schedule and the disorderly behavior of some students on the bus.

The withdrawal of a few students from suburban schools was directly linked to the unsafe and threatening condition of the bus.

2.2.5. Case Illustrations

Students who withdrew from the transfer program rarely cited a single determinative factor in their decision to withdraw. Most often, a combination of factors influenced the family's perception that the sacrifices of the transfer process outweighed the benefits.

One mother said her son discovered, "... there were a lot of cliques at school and my son wasn't really allowed to be part of them." Her son said, "White people would associate with you and talk with you but you could tell they were just playing around." Another parent withdrew her child because the new school could not cope with her son's behavioral problems. She went to school several times to talk with his teachers. This parent tried to encourage them to deal "forcefully" with her child and to "tell him what to do." "But," she said, "they didn't know how to deal with black children; they were manipulated by them. They definitely needed some orientation and training in how to deal with black children."

Racial prejudice figured prominently in some transfer students' decisions to withdraw. Most often, students reported that they experienced racial prejudice "in subtle ways": misunderstandings with teachers, references to racial stereotypes, and the perception that differential treatment was accorded to black and to white students. For one student it was a case of being embarrassed in front of peers: "He came home saying that the teachers out there were prejudiced. He felt that they were always trying to embarrass him in front of the class and that bothered him." Another family experienced prejudice on the part of both the students and teachers: "We were completely dissatisfied. We experienced a lot of racial prejudice among the students, name-calling for the most part. Also, we were very dissatisfied with the attitude of the teachers. The teachers basically had a 'deaf ear' to us whenever we tried to approach them to discuss our son."

Finally, transportation proved to be more of a burden than many families anticipated. One student said he suffered academically because of the late buses: "The buses were late and as a result I often missed parts of the school day. This, coupled with the fact that I was already behind, made it next to impossible for me to keep up." Two mothers related their frustrations with transportation problems: "The third week of school again the bus was either delayed or didn't show up at all! We were absolutely disgusted with this! We called the transportation office numerous times but it was busy all day long. Also, the principal of the school promised to have the situation corrected but it never was. When they weren't picked up we'd have to call a cab and then the kids wouldn't get there until 11 or 12. School is out at 2:45 p.m. Twice a week the bus was one to one and a half hours late bringing the kids home. They were also asked to switch buses at midyear."

2.3. CITY BLACK STUDENTS IN CITY SCHOOLS WHO PLAN TO TRANSFER

Students and parents in the following category are of city families who applied for interdistrict transfer for the school year 1983-84. A stay was ordered by the federal court early in the school year that prevented this group from enrolling in suburban schools until 1984-85. The vast majority of these respondents report acceptance by a suburban district and plans to transfer in September 1984. This group offers an important perspective because it is most in touch with the fears and expectations of prospective transfer students.

Two student and two parent focus groups constituted the panel discussion portion of this category. The adult groups involved the participation of three parents each. Eleven students from grades 4 to 7 participated in their group sessions.

Twenty-four telephone interviews supplemented the initial response elicited from focus group participants; 80 percent of the respondents were adults, of whom 85 percent were female.

2.3.1. Reasons for Application for Interdistrict Transfer

The city black students who signed up to transfer to suburban schools but who still matriculated in city schools presented a fuller picture of the multiple reasons why students wish to transfer. Some students were pulled toward suburban schools because they or their parents genuinely believed that they would get a better education there. They believed this because parents thought the teachers were less overwhelmed with large classes and discipline problems and, therefore, could give more attention to the individual needs of students. Also, some parents wish their offspring to experience a more racially integrated learning environment. Beyond these perceived attractions of the suburban schools for city students, some students were pushed away from the city because of bad social influences, disruptive and disorderly behavior of students at school, and personal conflicts.

Deficient instructional materials and crowded city classrooms were sometimes mentioned, as well as apathetic teachers. But these reasons were mentioned less often than environmental circumstances such as unruly behavior, particularly swearing and fighting, as influences that propel students away from city schools.

We stated that students still enrolled in city schools awaiting transfer to the county are an interesting group to study because they have committed themselves to transfer but have not taken decisive action that may require justification. Indeed, the opinions of some of the students currently in city schools reveal that they would prefer to remain where they are but have been urged to seek participation in the interdistrict program by their parents, teachers, or counselors. On balance, one may conclude that city students are pushed away from city schools more than they are pulled toward county schools. This fact means that the city can exercise a measure of control over the decisions of their students to leave the city system by undertaking deliberate efforts to improve it.

2.3.2. Expectations for Suburban Schools

Prospective transfer students and their parents were questioned about what they expected to be the major differences between the city schools and the suburban districts to which they were preparing to transfer. Almost all respondents expect improved educational opportunities as a result of the transfer. Typically, they refer to better facilities: cleaner, brighter, newer buildings, an unlimited stock of school supplies, more richly endowed athletic and activity facilities, and better food in the lunchroom.

Transfer families also expect better teaching in their new suburban districts. Allusions to "nicer" and "smarter" teachers were made by children. Smaller class sizes were also anticipated by city transfers.

Some city families had lived in suburban communities before and they expected suburban schools to be now as they were then. However, not all city residents perceive a link between quality education and suburban schooling. Some would be pleased to remain in the city if city schools were upgraded.

33

2.3.3. Liabilities of Transfer to Suburban Schools

City students and their parents also were aware of the possible liabilities associated with enrollment in a county school and expressed them in group discussion sessions. They labeled the transportation problems about which they had heard a great deal as a real hardship. Moreover, they expressed fear of losing their neighborhood friends and, simultaneously, failing to make any new acquaintances among whites in suburban schools. The small number of black families in the suburbs was spoken of as a liability too.

2.3.4. Threatening City Influences

The potential liabilities of the transfer process were not of sufficient magnitude to deter city parents from attempting to escape some influences of the urban community that they also characterized as negative. They were described sometimes as "bad company" that distracted city students from studying. Alluded to most frequently was the "cussing, pushing, shoving, and fighting" in city schools. Such behavior was unacceptable to many students as well as to their parents, who took advantage of the transfer program to avoid these negative influences. Thus, many city students remained on the waiting list for an opportunity to transfer to the suburbs.

2.4. BLACK RESIDENTS OF THE CITY ATTENDING MAGNET SCHOOLS

This section documents the perceptions of black students and parents who reside in the City of Saint Louis and who are enrolled in one of the magnet schools. Two focus groups were convened for this category, a group of five parents and another of three students. These groups were supplemented by four phone interviews; in all, this represented the experiences of six males and six females. The students attend Visual and Performing Arts, Math and Science, Career Education, Montessori, Stix, Wilkinson, Ames, Military, Mason, Academic and Athletic Academy, and other magnet schools.

2.4.1. Learning Environment

A principal reason for enrolling in city magnet schools for these families was the perceived opportunity for a better education and more discipline in these settings. Parents said that the disruptive behavior characteristic of some of the regular schools is not present in the magnet schools. The students said that there is strict enforcement of rules: "You can't cut class." Parents said, "teachers are

34

quick to contact the home, if there is a problem." In general, parents and students gave magnet teachers and their schools high marks. Students said that they were treated with respect by most magnet-school teachers.

Parents and students both appeared to be satisfied with race relations in magnet schools. They asserted that there are no discernible patterns of race-related tensions among students. However, some black students felt that white suburban students were "stuck in their own group." They said that whites were inclined to develop close friendships with other whites, especially in schools that were predominantly black. Several parents said that they were pleased with the interracial balance in magnet schools. A few parents claimed that there were subtle forms of discrimination in student-teacher interactions, but they did not elaborate. A few white students complained of aggressive behavior by blacks. In general, however, racial encounters were harmonious.

Students said that teaching at the magnet schools, especially among teachers in specialty subjects, is better than at regular schools. When necessary, teachers give individualized instruction. With reference to facilities, parents and students were unhappy with the condition of the magnet school buildings, books, supplies, and laboratory equipment. Some were concerned about the upkeep of school buildings too. An additional concern expressed by many students was the absence of after-school activities, and particularly athletic activities, at most magnet schools.

In general, city black residents applauded the magnet schools as moving public education in the right direction and recommended that the program be expanded. Some had returned to the public schools from private schools because of the presence of magnet schools.

2.4.2. Parent Participation

Parents of black magnet school students who reside in the city expressed a high level of interest in their children's schools. They feel a certain sense of frustration, though, in not being able to communicate more directly with the Board of Education, although they are pleased with the direct communication they have with teachers. They identified important issues regarding the differential resource levels of schools within the city system. They feel this is a part of the legacy of the dual school system which existed prior to the court's intervention in 1979. They also assailed the length of the waiting list for black students who have applied to magnet schools. Black families believed they deserve access to what they feel are the system's best schools. These are the issues that they feel need to be articulated to the Board but they have no vehicle at their disposal to do so.

Some black parents of students in magnet schools are also discouraged by the low participation rate of black parents in school-related activities. These parents believed that other parents should be more informed about their children's progress in school.

Parents and students exuded a sense of pride and accomplishment in being affiliated with a city magnet school. They are aware of the number of students waiting for seats to open up in the magnet programs, and those families who have been admitted feel a special distinction. Parents of black students enrolled in city magnet schools displayed a great deal of pride in their children's accomplishments. They reported that they, as parents, must spend a great deal of time and energy in supporting their children through the challenges of a rigorous academic program.

2.4.3. Case Illustrations

Black students and their parents support the magnet school program. Regarding the school as a learning environment, a black elementary student said, "Mama said the magnet school is better." One student said the magnet school students are "more disciplined ... the kids don't act crazy." "Students are not wild," is the way another student characterized her magnet-school classmates. Yet these schools are characterized as less rigid. One parent said, "the magnet school teachers are supportive of the kids." Another mother was so impressed that she said the "magnet concept should include preschool and day-care centers."

In terms of race relations, one black student said, "My friends are both black and white." A black mother said, "There are no racial tensions." The presence of "black role models" is what another parent liked about city magnet schools. That parent was also "delighted with the racial balance" at her child's school. In general, black parents said that black and white children in magnet schools "seem to get along well."

The physical condition of magnet schools is a nagging problem. A

36

black father said that this contributed to "a serious image problem."
A shortage of "laboratory and learning facilities" was the complaint
of another father. A student who is loyal to magnet schools and
who had attended several said, "Facilities in the magnet schools
are just about the same as those in the regular schools." She talked
about the "raggedy desks" and "little equipment in the chemistry
lab" and "not enough books to go around."

Although most students liked their magnet schools, a few thought
it good that students in such schools "don't get 'souped up' by the
coaches"; but many wished for "more sports and more after-school
activities, especially at the high school level" and "better gym facilities."

2.5. REACTION OF SUBURBAN BLACK RESIDENTS TO CITY BLACK STUDENTS

What follows is a discussion of issues relevant to the experience
of black students and parents of students who reside in the suburbs
and attend school with black city transfer students. This is an engag-
ing perspective as it represents the relationship of families of the
same race but who come from, in some cases, significantly different
social situations.

This category is composed of twenty-two respondents. Four parents
and five students gathered in two separate focus-group sessions.
The balance of the response was elicited by telephone interviews.
Over two-thirds (73 percent) of respondents were female.

The discussion group leader of black suburban residents characterized
their reaction to city black students in suburban schools as "ambivalent." The black suburban residents had to reassess their position
in school and community as a result of the presence of other blacks
new to the local suburban system.

The black suburban residents knew that some prejudice surrounded
them. However, they had made what they believed to be a reasonable
adaptation. With the coming of an increased number of blacks,
racial prejudice of some whites became overt and sometimes was
directed toward suburban black residents as well as black city transfer
students. Some black suburban students were disappointed with
their white friends and the residual prejudice they had maintained.
Others were annoyed with black city students whose presence evoked
these negative feelings on the part of whites.

2.5.1. Ambivalence of Suburban Blacks to City Blacks

The ambivalence of some black suburban residents resulted from a sense of confusion about whom they should blame for their increased discomfort, the whites who continued to harbor feelings of racial prejudice (although previously it had been less apparent), or the city blacks whose presence in the suburbs stimulated the emergence of these alleged prejudicial feelings by whites. These were two kinds of reactions by suburban blacks to the presence of city blacks in predominantly white suburban schools.

Other suburban blacks turned toward the black newcomers from the city and tried to help. They welcomed them and were pleased that others were present to press the issues about which they had struggled for recognition in the past. Still others rejected the newcomers as people who, they believed, made life more difficult for all blacks because they could not or would not try to fit in.

Finally some suburban blacks were inclined neither to accept or reject city blacks. They more or less assumed the position of neutral observers. Neutrality, however, was hard to maintain because many whites often lumped all blacks together and refused to make distinctions between suburban and city blacks.

2.5.2. Social/Class Distinctions

Black suburban residents often explained differences between their patterns of adaptations to suburban schools and those of city black students as a function of their different social/class positions. Thus, some of the hostility of suburban blacks to city blacks may be based on the social stratification system. Suburban blacks who reject other blacks because of social class accuse the city black youngsters of making a lot of noise and dressing in unacceptable ways. They refer to city black students "as defeated people who do not care," students who tend "not to talk in class," who act as if they were "dumb." They single out city black boys in particular and describe their behavior as "loud and rambunctious," and say that they are quick to fight. Generally such students are described as having "a chip on their shoulders." Suburban blacks are bothered by the assumption of city black kids that all blacks who live in the suburbs are rich.

2.5.3. Racial Solidarity

Suburban blacks who choose to identify with other students of the same race seek alliance with city black students. They offer to serve as host families for city students, keep under surveillance the appointment practices of the school system with reference to positions on athletic teams and cheering squads and other extracurricular activities, and pressure the suburban schools to acknowledge black history through black awareness weeks.

2.5.4. Student Adjustment: An Interracial Responsibility

The black suburban families who are more or less neutral about the presence of black city students in their suburban school systems probably represent the greater proportion of blacks in such settings. They describe the adjustment problems of city blacks in suburban settings as a function of how whites and blacks interact as well as how the two populations isolate themselves from each other. They describe some of their white peers as trying too hard to relate to blacks by awkwardly giving "black handshakes" and trying to use black idiomatic expressions. They see white teachers who repeatedly forget that black suburban resident students are not city transfer students. They realize that some city black students perceive all suburban students as white, including suburban black students, and do not believe that blacks can be friends both with black and with white students. They see principals as having a major impact on how well the new students are received. They believe that get-togethers between city and suburban residents will ease the process of adaptation of both groups to each other. They see the adaptation of blacks in suburban school systems as a function both of race and of social class; further, they realize that some city black students are ahead and others are behind their suburban classmates academically.

The above analysis indicates that the reaction to and relationship between city black students and suburban black students is most complicated. A hasty analysis is likely to lead to an oversimplification of a multifaceted relationship. There is a range of adaptations that must be considered, as this discussion has indicated.

2.5.5. Case Illustrations

In trying to determine who is to blame for their discomfort pertaining to suburban school desegregation, a black suburban student said, "Some kids came out here with chips on their shoulders." Another said, "White people are afraid the blacks are going to 'take over.'" Still another student accused the city blacks of "not trying hard enough" or of "being prejudiced against white people." This diagnosis was opposed by a suburban black student who found whites to be "insensitive to city blacks and basically misunderstanding them." City black students were accused of "staying to themselves" and not trying to fit in with the mainstream, by some suburban blacks. Others said, however, that the city black students try to join organizations in the suburbs but are excluded by an informal quota system. He said, "There are only two black students on each team."

A black suburban parent described city black students as "independent." "They like to do things on their own and not listen." This behavior, she said, "is going to get one of them into trouble." However, another suburban black parent observed that "the absence of black teachers in suburban schools is the real problem for the black city kids." Some black instructors in suburban schools were described by another parent as having to "stand back and look at these things and grit their teeth, this is the politics of the situation."

This episode of insensitivity was reported by a black suburban parent. She said, "The principal felt that a black history assembly would make the blacks in suburban schools feel separated and that they didn't need it. He felt that an assembly on black history would foster segregation. The black students told the principal that they wanted to let white students be aware of how they felt. So this year was the first year that black history was celebrated in that school." A teacher helped the black kids put on the assembly, said the parent, "but he didn't have the principal's support." Another black suburban parent concluded that "the only way most black students can face and eliminate stereotypes and racial prejudice is for the administration to support and reach out to these students." "Some kids get so frustrated," said one parent, that "they become like a mad bull and then they get what they want." This is always a problem, suburban black parents agreed, "when the control is vested in whites." Another black parent chimed in, "I'm training my kid to protect herself because I'm not there all the time."

A suburban black father resented the suggestion that the city black students ought to receive special attention. He said, "I'm in an all-white corporation. I'm no different from anyone else. I had to fight for myself. I moved on my own worth. The kids have to take responsibility. They're going to have to conform." Then he said that his child reported that some of the city black kids "are running around with a lot of money, buying drugs." He told of a success story about a black student from the city who learned how to conform and who now "is an honor student and is real happy to be going to school in the suburbs." Another father continued, "I can't buy that the kids coming out here are not prepared. They are prepared to learn. It's the instructors who are not prepared to teach. Some county teachers let the city kids say and do anything because they believe the city black kids are a different caliber from the suburban kids."

CHAPTER THREE

PERCEPTIONS OF WHITE STUDENTS AND PARENTS

This chapter on the perspective of white students documents the experience of active county-to-city magnet school transfer students, former magnet school transfers who have chosen to withdraw from the city program and return to their home suburban districts, and white residents of the city in magnet schools. Again, the observations of both parents and students are included in the discussions of what were judged by the respondents to be the most salient issues related to the transfer experience.

3.1. SUBURBAN WHITE STUDENTS WHO TRANSFERRED TO AND REMAINED IN MAGNET SCHOOLS

This section describes the academic and interpersonal experiences of students who made the decision to transfer from their public or private schools in Saint Louis County to a city magnet school program. Also reported are perceived deficiencies, according to suburban participants. This information should prove useful to educators committed to a strong and stable magnet school program.

Two parent and two student focus groups were organized to address the issues specific to the magnet school program. A total of nine parents (three fathers, six mothers) represented the adult component of this category. Two student groups, one with three fourth-graders and a second with five ninth-graders described student experiences with the magnet program.

These initial findings were followed up by a series of thirty-eight phone interviews with magnet school transfers from the suburbs. Just over half of these respondents (53 percent) were active magnet school students and the majority of these were high-school transfers. Adult respondents were primarily parents of children too young to give the interviewer a detailed response.

42

3.1.1. Reasons for Transfer

Suburban parents and students involved in the city magnet program report that the special curriculum in magnet schools is the primary appeal of this program. Some gifted students report being bored by the standard academic repertoire of their home districts. Others with interests in the arts, ROTC, and the classics have few opportunities to fulfill these interests in suburban schools.

Some families withdraw their children from their home districts in response to an administrative decision that they resent. Students have reported that their possible suspension, disputes with teachers, or conflicts with classmates have prompted some families to withdraw from the suburban schools and enroll in a magnet school program.

Other students and parents suggest that they were pushed from their home districts in some instances, because of the perceived racial and social-class homogeneity and parochialism of some suburban schools. County residents have alluded to their unhappiness with the striking racial imbalance of certain suburban school systems. Hence, they have turned to city magnet schools for exposure to ethnic diversity.

It is fair to say that county students who enroll in city magnet schools are pulled to these learning environments by appealing curricular opportunities and the possibility of desegregated education more so than they are pushed away from their home districts because of dissatisfaction.

3.1.2. Quality of Instruction

White students in city magnet schools describe some of their teachers as exceptionally committed and in command of their subject areas. These teachers were described as offering challenging courses. They gave liberally of their time to students and, in some cases, used their personal resources to compensate for insufficient school supplies. The students also described most magnet school teachers as fair. In general, parents felt that their children were getting a good education at city magnet schools.

Despite high marks given to most magnet school teachers, suburban white parents and students were quite critical of the condition of the physical plant in which magnet schools were housed. They spoke of peeling paint, falling plaster, poorly maintained restrooms, and inadequate cafeteria services.

County students complain that some of their city peers in magnet schools are not interested in the area of specialization in which they have enrolled. They allege that some city students attend magnet schools in order to escape the difficulties of the regular schools.

These differences are real. Suburban white students who volunteer to enroll in city magnet schools remain enthusiastic about the uniqueness of their institutions. County transfers described their classmates at magnet schools as not snobbish and more tolerant of a range of lifestyles. They displayed pride in their schools and were quick to defend them and recommend ways for their improvement. They also encouraged their siblings and suburban friends to consider transfer.

3.1.3. Socialization and Race Relations

Suburban white students commented that they experienced difficulty in making friends when they first enrolled in city magnet schools, but eventually overcame any feelings of estrangement. One student described her school as fun and exciting. Her attitude was representative of several students. Others said they had no problem interacting with black students during the school day but were reluctant to visit their new classmates in their homes. They described the all-black neighborhoods as threatening and off-limits to whites. For these reasons, interaction between city and suburban students was limited largely to the regular school day.

White students and their parents both report a strong record of racial harmony within the magnet schools. No discernible pattern of race-related hostility was observed among students. Students, however, detected a serious level of racial bias among faculty members. Suburban transfer students alleged that a number of black teachers were openly hostile to their presence in the city system, believing they were crowding out black students who deserved a magnet school education. Magnet schools were obligated to reserve a substantial proportion of their seats for white students.

Racism also emerged as an important concern in the home suburban districts of the magnet-school students. Suburban white neighbors and friends of these students were openly critical of their decision to attend school with blacks in the city. In a few cases, students lost jobs and friends as a result of their participation in the magnet school program. Suburban residents were also critical of the magnet chool students' allegedly wasteful use of tax dollars to pay for magnet school students' commute to the city. They described such use as wasteful. This criticism was especially virulent when discussing he use of taxi cabs for interdistrict transfer.

Students also report that some counselors and other administrators were reluctant to support or facilitate a transfer. In several instances, suburban parents have reported difficulty in securing the transfer of records required for admission to magnet schools.

3.1.4. Persisting Problems

Both students and parents who lived in the suburbs were of the opinion that the greatest threat to the viability of the magnet component of the interdistrict transfer program is the poor physical condition of the city schools. They report that the buildings were poorly maintained and are not pleasant learning environments.

Suburban magnet students complained of the length of their school day, due largely to the distance they had to travel from their suburban homes. Some also were critical of the prejudiced attitudes expressed by cab drivers. These students were lectured by drivers on the danger of the inner city and the wasteful expenditure of public funds for school desegregation.

Parents have been highly critical of the sites chosen for some magnet schools. They have threatened not to allow their children to attend a school if it is located in a "dangerous neighborhood." They felt that more appropriate sites should have been chosen. Some county residents wanted magnet schools placed in the suburbs; others said such locations would be unfair to city students and contrary to the spirit of equity of the settlement plan.

3.1.5. Case Illustrations

For county residents, the process of transferring to a city magnet school includes a variety set of perceived benefits and concerns. Most stated that their reasons for transferring are centered in search of a "specialized academic program" that meets the needs of individual children. A smaller number of parents and students discussed the perceived racial and social homogeneity of the suburbs as a factor that contributed to their desire to find another more heterogeneous educational setting.

45

One student was quick to share the negative reaction of her suburban neighbors to her transfer to a magnet school: "I had a lot of friends who were prejudiced and I don't talk to them anymore because when they found out I was going to a city school they just thought, oh God, you've lost your mind."

Another student described how her magnet school transfer affected her social life: "My neighbors wouldn't talk to me; I used to babysit their little boy all the time; they wouldn't let me do it; they called me and said we're not going to let you babysit anymore because you go to a school that's filled with niggers. I just hung up the phone."

Once enrolled in the magnet school, students and parents expressed a different set of concerns. County residents transferring to magnet schools found their teachers to be, in general, "qualified" and "concerned." By contrast, the physical conditions of the magnet schools are a source of concern to many parents.

Magnet school students from the county find their fellow students to be "friendly" and "accessible." There were few reports of racial tension involving students. It was more common for students to report perceptions of racial bias among faculty members. One white parent commented that her daughter reported that "she had one teacher this year who she had a problem with and it was racial. The teacher openly favored black girls over everyone else." Another parent recognized a similar pattern in her child's experiences: "The only thing I noticed in two years with my youngest daughter is that the black girls are the least accepting. She had several black boys who were friends and went to a couple of school picnics with her new friends. She noticed that in these outings the black girls would all be in one bunch and the black boys and white girls and white boys all played together. The black girls were a closed group."

A father explained his family's rationale for interdistrict transfer: "We didn't look at it as having anything to do with racial mix, we looked at it as another kind of educational opportunity that was available." This point of view was supported by a fellow transfer parent: "I don't think there were ever any racial incidents racially motivated, some fights and rumors spread like in any school, but they were not racial."

Persistent problems for these students include lengthy daily schedules, inadequate physical facilities, prejudiced cab drivers, and the placement of magnet schools in what they consider to be dangerous neighborhoods. Despite these drawbacks, most students expressed pride and enthusiasm when discussing their schools.

3.2. SUBURBAN WHITE STUDENTS WHO WITHDREW FROM MAGNET SCHOOLS

Like their black counterparts in the city-to-county transfer program who have withdrawn from the suburban schools, this group of magnet school withdrawals highlighted the most visible weaknesses of their former program. This category presented several difficulties for the project staff in its attempt to enlist participation of white students and parents in focus groups. Many expressed disaffection with the magnet program and believed participation in a focus group would amount to a show of support for the transfer program. Therefore, this category is heavily dependent on data from phone interviews for parent and student feedback.

Two focus groups with a total of six former county-to-city magnet students shared their opinions and experiences during panel discussions. These students were from mixed grade levels, ranging from the fourth to ninth grades. An insufficient number of white parents agreed to participate in an adult focus group.

Thirty-seven suburban white parents and students who had at one time attended city magnet schools were reached by phone. Roughly two-thirds of these (69 percent) were adults, the vast majority (88 percent) being female adults living at home.

3.2.1. Curriculum

White students who withdrew from the magnet school program and who returned to their home districts expressed disappointment with the magnet schools' academic programs. They argued that there is no noticeable advantage to the transfer; in their judgment, the schools are not magnetized. They concluded that the sacrifices required of magnet school transfers were not justified in the light of program offerings. Though sometimes satisfied with the magnet school program's area of emphasis, they said they were not challenged by other courses. Students were also frustrated by the scarcity of extracurricular activities. Several reported returning to the suburbs in order to take advantage of sports and other after-school activities.

Teacher layoffs and severely deferred capital improvement projects

47

have adversely affected the magnet school program and, in certain cases, prompted the withdrawal of suburban transfers. The teachers' strike at the start of the 1983-84 school year was also an unsettling experience and contributed to the dissatisfaction experienced by suburban white students who withdrew from the interdistrict transfer program.

3.2.2. School Climate

Suburban students enrolled in city magnet schools have described their teachers and fellow students as representing a wide range of talent. Those who withdrew from the magnet school program were unhappy with such a range. Some had expected greater selectivity. This disappointment was particularly evident among suburban white students who felt their own academic progress was being impeded.

Withdrawing students were critical of the administrative and teaching staff in magnet schools, too. A careful analysis of these perceptions revealed, on the one hand, a breakdown in communication between teachers and students of different racial and cultural traditions and, on the other, the presence of prejudice and stereotyping. These students accused some principals of precipitating conflict among school professionals; some teachers were charged with harboring prejudicial attitudes toward whites.

3.2.3. Transportation

Suburban white students and parents experienced some frustration with the inefficiences of the transportation system. They raise the same issues as were discussed by city students who transferred to the county schools: unreliable bus routing, complaints about drivers, and mechanical breakdown of vehicles. Though some students experienced ten-hour days due to the distance they had to travel and complained about the excessive time devoted to transportation, the distance factor alone was usually not reason enough to prompt withdrawal. Typically, it was mentioned in connection with other unsatisfactory experiences as the basis for returning to the suburban home district. In summary, most withdrawals were due to compounded circumstances rather than to a single deficiency.

3.2.4. Case Illustrations

This section includes perceptions of students and parents who had

48

previously participated in the county-to-city magnet-school transfer program but who have since withdrawn. These respondents reportedly expected a stronger curriculum in the magnet school program and were consequently disappointed if some element of the schools, either the basic curriculum or the specialized program of emphasis, did not measure up.

One student expressed disappointment with the "general quality" of the magnet program: "My expectations were not met at all. I was only given one art class. The teachers and the quality of the materials were inferior to those in regular suburban schools." A father felt that "although pleased with the magnet part of the program, the regular courses (the three R's) just couldn't compare with the suburban district." Several students returned to suburban schools to pursue extracurricular interests unavailable at the magnet schools: "My son was reluctant to leave the magnet school but did so in order to play football."

In some cases, parents found the range of talent, both in the faculty and in the student body, to be too wide. Implicit here was an expectation of greater selectivity in terms of student interest and skill level, as well as professional expertise and commitment. A mother whose son had attended a magnet school compared it with his suburban experience: "Our child basically got the impression that the magnet school was very disorganized, and did very little in the way of attempting to make white students feel welcome. Frankly, our local suburban district is a notch or two better than the city schools." Another parent was unhappy because "my child was not being challenged." She believed that many of her child's classmates were not as advanced as in the suburban schools. Also she was "disappointed because the school did not offer a computer class."

Students who chose to withdraw from the magnet schools reported that in the final analysis the difficulty required to effect transfer (transportation, threatened peer network, limited extracurricular opportunities) was not worth the sacrifice, so they returned to resident suburban districts or to a private school. Students offered an array of explanations for their magnet school withdrawals: "Transportation was a real problem. Buses failed to show up occasionally. Cabs were late. Kids on the buses were rowdy. Some didn't like riding buses at all." A student said, "I had very long days, picked up early in the morning and came home late in the afternoon." Another complaint was, "I felt that the curriculum was rather weak in general areas and did not prepare me adequately for college. I also thought that the counseling was very poor." A student added, "Basically, the major reason I decided to withdraw was that the school went downhill as a result of loss of funding. While I was very enthusiastic about the school at first, as the school lost funding it began to layoff many of my favorite teachers." A mother related that "the main sacrifices that my daughter had to make were in the social area. She felt that she lost touch with her friends in the neighborhood and felt 'out of it' in terms of what was going on in the local suburban community."

3.3. WHITE RESIDENTS OF THE CITY IN MAGNET SCHOOLS

This section portrays the experience of white residents of the city of Saint Louis who have chosen to enroll in one of the system's magnet schools. Theirs is an interesting perspective for a number of reasons. First, they have witnessed the adaptation process experienced by suburban white students who attend magnet schools as part of the county-to-city transfer program. Second, they are qualified to comment on the general quality of their specialized educational opportunities. And third, because the magnet schools maintain a racial balance for both faculty and students, these students and parents offer a unique view of the nature of race relations in these schools. All ten respondents contributing to this section were contacted by phone.

White students from the city who attend magnet schools expressed a sense of overall satisfaction with their schools. They report, with pride, a perception that the magnet schools provide the student a high quality academic program as well as a racially integrated environment. Therefore, they wish for more of such schools. Mothers are "pleased" with magnet schools; students are "stimulated" in them; magnet school teachers are "enthusiastic." This is the report card of praise that magnet schools receive from white parents and their offspring who live in the city.

3.3.1. Quality of Education

Perhaps the first and most compelling issue raised by city white parents and students alike was the contrast, in terms of educational quality, between the regular city schools and the magnet schools. The magnet schools are believed to be of a generally higher caliber than other city public schools. The students are described as more disciplined because the schools "really mean business." The curriculum is perceived to be better. Rules are enforced in ways that are thought to be fair. Teachers appear to be more committed to the students and are willing to communicate with parents.

While white magnet school students and parents believe that their schools are better, physically many of these schools are in need of repair. Also, better maintenance would help improve them as learning environments. Parents and students commented on the need for laboratory equipment, paint, plaster, general cleanliness, additional textbooks, and more.

White parents and students believe that high-quality education in the magnet schools is the result of the specialized academic program. They believe that the learning environment is greatly enhanced by a sense of focus and common interest among faculty and students. They appreciate the concept of the "magnet," which draws students who want to, rather than are required to, attend a given school.

3.3.2. Race Relations

Several parents of white city residents attending magnet schools discussed an integrated racial environment as one of the reasons for enrolling their children in magnet schools. Exposure to a multi-cultural setting, as well as a guaranteed racial balance, was believed to enhance children's learning.

Parents were pleased by the perceived absence of racial tension in city magnet schools. Several parents expressed their hope that exposure to other races would result in open-minded children and, eventually, less biased adults. Some magnet schools, however, have a way to go before they reach the goals mentioned above. Even though the schools are integrated, some white parents noticed that their children tend to select other whites as close friends. One parent thought that this practice may be due to subtle racism. One student felt uncomfortable in his magnet school because whites were a minority of the total student body.

3.3.3. General Curriculum

While most parents expressed satisfaction with the curriculum and academic rigor of the magnet schools, a few parents are concerned that the nonspecialized subjects need more attention. Some parents, especially parents of elementary school children, questioned the "excessive field trips." These criticisms, however, were less frequent than the praise that white parents had for city magnet schools. In addition to the above concerns, some parents wished that magnet schools were equipped with better sports and gymnasium facilities.

3.3.4. Case Illustrations

A middle-school student said that the "accelerated program" in which she participated is very "stimulating." Her mother said she is very "happy with the program and would change absolutely nothing." Another mother with a son in a magnet school said her son is "learning a lot" and that she cannot think of any changes to suggest.

The parents who praised the magnet schools as good learning environments also appreciated them as settings that contribute to their children's understanding of different cultures. "My children will gain the open-mindedness which they would not attain in neighborhood schools," is the way one parent stated the case for interracial contact. Another reported an observation by her son: "everything is 50/50 and there are no racists." Much of the good racial climate was attributed to teachers "who treat you with respect," said a tenth-grade white student.

Clearly, the white students who attend city magnet schools want a comprehensive education, one that is racially integrated and of high quality. They appeared to be pleased because they are getting both in the Saint Louis magnet schools. The parent whose children returned from private schools to the public school system demonstrates this comprehensive interest: "Our kids attend magnet schools because the emphasis is academic. We took our kids out of a private school because it was too expensive. This is the third magnet school they have attended. We wanted to stay in the city schools so that our kids will be exposed to a racial mix. The children appear to be more serious in magnet schools."

3.4. REACTION OF WHITE SUBURBAN PARENTS AND STUDENTS TO BLACK CITY TRANSFER STUDENTS

This section is a treatment of what were presented as important issues for white students and parents who reside in the suburbs and attend school with city transfer students. It is considered a vital perspective since reaction by receiving students and parents so often sets the tone of the transfer student's experience. It also greatly influences the new students' adjustment process and the likelihood of their developing a sense of belonging in their new school districts.

Twenty-six parents and students contributed to this dimension of the project. Two parent groups of five and seven met to discuss how the transfer program is working in their districts. One student group of four middle school students described their experiences as classmates of city transfer students. Ten other subjects (eight students) were contacted by phone.

3.4.1. Assessment of Program

White parents do not hesitate to assert that their support of the voluntary plan is in large measure out of fear that the Court will order more drastic measures. Put simply, suburban white families in metropolitan Saint Louis have a strong allegiance to their local school districts. Many move to their particular subdivisions because of the reputation of the local schools and do not want to risk the chance of being bused away from them. The result has been a conscientious effort on the part of the suburban white residents to make the plan work. The issue of local control is indirectly raised by parents who state that it is unfair for city students to have the benefit of a quality suburban education without paying for it.

Some parents participate in host family programs and act as sponsors for the black city students. Those who participate in school activities are more favorable to the interdistrict tranfer program than families that do not do so. Even when families are negative toward the program, they often attempt to shield their attitudes; they believe the interdistrict voluntary transfer program is preferable to a mandatory interdistrict school desegregation plan. Thus, most negative attitudes expressed by suburban parents have to do with the financing of the plan. A common response is that the money spent on transportation should be spent on the city schools.

Though most suburban whites support the program, their support is qualified by an insistence that their own children not be crowded out of special programs. They believe that their responsibility is to prevent the watering down of the curriculum and related learning programs. In the process of expressing their concern about the quality of the educational experience during the first year of the interdistrict transfer program, some racial stereotypes that suburban whites have of blacks surface. They believe city blacks are less well prepared academically than suburban white students and that they may find the learning environment in the suburbs tougher. They believe that their suburban school districts may be tempted to lower their standards to accommodate city students, and they expect city black students to present greater disciplinary problems. When pressed to assess the interdistrict school desegregation process, however, most suburban white parents respond that it has gone well and that there

53

are no real problems. This is especially the assessment from parents who have been involved in the program as host families or in some other capacity.

3.4.2. Student Adjustment Patterns

The students observed that black boys and white boys were much more successful in getting along together than were their female peers. The children surmised that this was due to the nature of the activities in which the boys participated. The boys were more inclined to participate in sports than were the girls. Extracurricular activities were mentioned as an important way of bringing the racial populations together.

Some students tried to make the city students feel "at home" when they came to the suburbs. Some acted as hosts and guides during orientation sessions. Some white females turned toward black males because, as stated by their white peers, "it was a cool thing to do." Others, including males and females, were genuinely attracted to blacks as new friends and did not make distinctions between students by race.

Some whites, however, opposed the presence of black transfer students in their public schools. They said the city blacks were "too loud" and "played by different rules." Some suburban parents believed that it was an unkind act of "cultural shock" to invite a city black student into an affluent white suburban home. The stereotypes that suburban white residents had of city black students were sometimes of extreme opposites. Some declared that most city transfer students were behind white suburban students in achievement while others accused the interdistrict program of draining off the brightest and best from city schools. In general, city black students were expected to conform to the ethos of their new suburban school systems. During the first year of the interdistrict transfer program it was reported that most city blacks in suburban schools kept a low profile.

3.4.3. Case Illustrations

The indirect support that white suburban parents give to the interdistrict program is illustrated by the remarks of this mother: "All of my friends are taking the attitude that all students should be given the opportunity to get a good education. Many of us do not agree with the way it's being funded with the extra expense, but at the same time the children do need the education and we want them in our school district if they can come up to standards which the school district has got both in education and discipline. Thus far, I have not seen a problem in our school district."

Demonstrating how direct participation and extracurricular activities contribute to transfer student acceptance, a white parent said of her son: "He really got a kick out of the city kids. A lot of them were a lot more fun to be around than his regular friends. He played athletics with the transfer students. We hosted them on game night after school up until game time and they were a delight to be around." This family had very positive impressions of their new friends from the city.

The city students are intriguing to some of the suburban students who have had limited contact with blacks. A parent explained that their daughter "chose as a subject for painting one of the black boys on the basketball team. She found him to be such an interesting person. I found it quite interesting that she should chose a black student as her first subject, as her first portrait." Others, however, find the black students threatening. A white middle school student said, "The city people are different from the county; they have different ways and different ideas of friendship. They can be trouble." A white mother expressed the fear "that behavior problems would accompany the city kids." She said, "parents were afraid that the black kids would 'hit first' and not talk through problems."

The reaction of whites to the presence of blacks in suburban areas is varied and ambivalent. They both accept and reject the transfer students. The kind of response a black student experiences has a great deal to do with the persons and the situations encountered. There was, however, a minimum of violence associated with the voluntary transfer of black students from the city to the suburbs in the Saint Louis metropolitan area. This peaceful adaptation was a normative response of the city and the suburbs to school desegregation that was commendable.

CHAPTER FOUR

PERCEPTIONS OF BLACK AND OF
WHITE PROFESSIONAL EDUCATORS

This chapter attempts to capture the professional perspective, primarily the reflections of teachers and school-based staff who had direct involvement with interdistrict transfer students in 1983-84. The first of our sections conveys the observations of city magnet-school teachers and their support-staff colleagues. Perceptions of suburban teachers and principals who had some form of involvement with city transfer students are related in the second section. Following this is a section on reflections by nonteaching personnel such as central office administrators, in most cases the district's superintendent of schools.

Data for the first two sections were drawn exclusively from focus-group sessions. The third section resulted from personal interviews conducted with officials.

4.1. CITY MAGNET SCHOOL EDUCATORS

Two focus groups involving thirteen magnet school teachers were held during the course of the project. Teachers represented eight different magnet schools and had an average of over twenty years of teaching experience. Eight of the thirteen teachers were black. Teachers addressed issues relevant to the county-to-city transfer program and more general quality of education topics.

4.1.1. Caliber of Student Body

Magnet school teachers in the Saint Louis Public Schools believe that they enjoy a fundamental advantage over colleagues from the regular schools in that their students make a conscious decision to attend their schools.

The magnet-school teachers also believe that the magnet programs are better than are programs in the regular schools. The magnet school teachers say they receive more cooperation from parents than do teachers in regular city schools. Their major criticism is that the subjects other than those emphasized in the school's speciality are not given the attention they deserve.

Despite these observations, magnet school teachers firmly believe that there is a major public misconception regarding the magnet schools. Most city residents presume that the magnet schools receive the most talented students and are favored with the best facilities and school-related resources. Teachers relate that class sizes are smaller than in some schools but are larger than they should be for specialized academic programs. They also report insufficient instructional materials and improperly designed facilities for the specific programs of emphasis.

Comparing city school life to that in suburban areas, magnet school teachers noted the greater range in skills and ability among teachers as well as students in the city. Teachers believe that stricter admissions standards for magnet schools are necessary to encourage a quality education. While they acknowledge that many magnet school students are high achievers, their major concern is the students of lesser ability who, they believe, impede the progress of others.

Many magnet school personnel feel that their schools are used as a last resort for some academic and behavioral problems from the suburban districts. Students from these settings frequently were referred to as "problem students" who were "dumped" on the city. Such attitudes contributed to a bind for some county residents. They were questioned by local suburban administrators regarding why they wished to transfer, ostracized by some neighbors for commuting to the city, and finally, stereotyped by some magnet school teachers as "problem" children.

Teachers believe that suburban transfer students are given the benefit of the doubt more often than city students in magnet schools when an infraction of the rules occurs. They believe that there is pressure on the city school district to maintain a high ratio of white students in magnet schools. This study did not investigate the validity of the allegation. It did detect a great deal of resentment, however, of the perceived practice.

4.1.2. Student Race Relations

Teachers are very positive regarding race relations among students at magnet schools. They portray a learning environment where little notice is given to race. Most teachers said there was little, if any, interracial hostility among students. They declared that desegregtion appears to be working in the magnet schools, although there still is a tendency for students of specific racial groups to sit with each other during lunchtime and a few awkward situations pertaining to interracial dating.

4.1.3. Teacher Morale

The primary source of racial friction in magnet schools, according to these teachers, is centered on the faculties. In severe cases, racial cleavages prevent coordinated action on the part of the magnet school teachers and contribute to the infighting and divisiveness that the students noted previously. The absence of a sense of community among city teachers is revealed in their racial estrangement. Many have anecdotes to share that are used to demonstrate the validity of their charges.

The bickering among teachers and lack of cooperation is sensed by students. Several magnet school students commented about the estranged relationships among teachers and between teachers and the administration.

4.1.4. Case Illustrations

The magnet school teachers with whom we met represented roughly half of the magnet schools and included both teachers of specialized subjects and teachers of general curriculum. They were very supportive of the magnet school program and articulated both the strengths and the areas of concern within the magnet schools.

According to the teachers, an advantage of the magnet schools is the fact that the students make a conscious decision to attend and are, on the whole, committed to their schools. Teachers reflected on the advantages of the magnet schools: "The children do their work, and seem to put forth more effort than the children in the regular schools." Also, "the parents seemed to back the teachers more" in the magnet schools. Another teacher commented on the "healthy school climate" that prevails at her school, saying,"In particular, the socialization process is very smooth at my school. There is extremely good rapport among the students, black and white, city and county." One teacher drew a distinction between the magnet school and regular programs saying, "a fundamental difference between magnet school children and regular-school children is that the magnet school children and/or their parents have made a conscious, specific decision to attend the magnet school."

They view as a misconception the idea that magnet schools receive the brightest students. The teachers discussed at length the varied skills and abilities of both magnet school students and teachers. In fact, their major criticism is that the subjects other than those emphasized in the school's speciality are not given the attention they deserve. When asked to share what they perceived to be the major weakness of the magnet school program, they related, "There is a fundamental misconception that magnet schools have the brightest students and the best materials and small class sizes; this simply is not the case." Another magnet school teacher noted, "A problem with the magnet school system is that the nature of the educational process at these schools is such that the students tend to get ahead in their focus areas and fall behind in general academic areas." Despite the absence of hostile interracial encounters, a teacher asserts that students are not prepared for the interracial classroom; "I believe a major deficiency is the absence of preparation for the integrated experience at the magnet schools. I introduced the idea at a meeting that some sort of orientation program whereby parents, students, and teachers involved in the desegregation plan are sensitized to the cultural differences between the races."

Other concerns expressed by magnet school teachers included their perception that suburban districts are sending many of their behavioral and academic problems to city magnet schools, and the fact that teacher morale is generally low. While race relations among students in the magnet schools were viewed positively, teachers reported racial tension among faculty members. One teacher shared a personal episode of racial tension: "One teacher allows other white teachers to use her classroom for after-school activities, but does not allow other black teachers to use it. Also black teachers have to be careful how they speak to this particular white teacher, who will often distort it to make the black teacher look bad." Another teacher explained the morale problem as a product of the high mobility of city teachers. "I feel the commitment of city teachers is lower because teachers get shuffled to different buildings; they have no loyalty to building or neighborhood."

Teacher morale is also affected by a perception that the magnet schools are receiving suburban, white students who were rejected by their suburban districts. "To a large extent the magnet schools in the city are a dumping ground for county kids with behavioral and/or disciplinary problems. Many of the county students are also low-caliber students in terms of their raw IQ," said a black city teacher. Regarding the socialization process, one teacher observed, "Many of the students from the county 'do not fit in' in their home districts because they tend to be, in one way or another, unconventional."

4.2. EDUCATORS FROM SUBURBAN DISTRICTS THAT RECEIVED CITY STUDENTS

Three focus groups with suburban personnel involved a total of twenty teachers, two counselors, one principal, and one school nurse. Teachers participating in this phase of the project had an average of approximately sixteen years of professional teaching experience, and only five reported to having experience outside of their present districts. Of the twenty-four participants, two were black.

This group reported on issues specific to the city transfer students' adjustment to their new suburban schools, their level of academic readiness, and their rate of progress over the course of their first year of enrollment. Also staff impressions were offered on the response of suburban districts to the desegregation plan and on the response of the white parents to the transfer program.

4.2.1. Skill Level of City Transfer Students

Suburban teachers who have had some form of experience with city blacks relate that these students represent a wide range of ability. Some of the students who are below grade level in one or more basic skills required at least a short period of remedial work.

Teachers also comment that city students are caught offguard by the high performance expectations of their new schools and must work harder to establish effective study habits. Despite these concerns, suburban personnel are firm in their belief that the transfer students are learning; some have achieved impressive records.

4.2.2. Student Adjustment Strategies of Suburban Districts

The sixteen suburban-school systems offered a wide range of interventions in their attempts to facilitate the adjustment of transfer students. Some personnel lauded their districts for the thoughtfulness of their efforts to provide a smooth transition to integration. In fact, some felt as though their districts had gone overboard, resulting in staff being "workshopped out." At the other extreme were teachers who felt abandoned by their districts. They relate that no provision was made to acquaint them with the basic cultural differences between the races that affect classroom dynamics.

The multicultural workshops that were offered tended to focus on the more global issues of racial politics and prejudice. Teachers felt they ignored the more practical issues relevant to classroom activity. Teachers encourage whatever measures the districts can devise to improve the level of parental involvement among transfer families. Those with "host family" experience recommend it highly as an effective vehicle for parent participation in curricular and extracurricular programs.

4.2.3. Student Adjustment and Race Relations

Principals in the sessions stated that successful adjustment by transfer students and the avoidance of race-related confrontations are due to effective classroom leadership. Teachers set the tone for a positive integrative experience and in districts where it is happening, principals say that teachers deserve the credit.

The involvement of city black students in extracurricular activities is the most effective means of adjustment to these students' schools. Teachers note the strong correlation between student maladjustment and nonparticipation in after-school activities.

4.2.4. Transportation

From the teachers' perspective, the greatest difficulty associated with the unreliable transportation system is the classroom interruption that occurs with the late arrival of transfer students. Teachers observed that students are affected by the long bus ride. They are in unison in their belief that the transfer plan must adopt a more efficient routing system in order to maintain the program's reputation as a valuable educational opportunity.

4.2.5. Community Relations

Suburban staff portray the community posture toward desegregation in a variety of shades, depending on the district in question. In some, the issue is very quiet, relegated to the back burner in the shadow of more pressing local issues. In other districts the communities hold attitudes that range from skepticism to open hostility. Many are reportedly waiting for something to go wrong. In relation to this, teachers are regularly questioned by parents regarding noticeable changes in the academic or behavioral quality of the school since desegregation.

Though the issue has not resulted in any form of open conflict, teachers have expressed concern with the future. As the competition for scarce resources heats up with the addition of transfer students to the district rolls, teachers wonder how a resident will react if his or her child is denied a place in an activity in favor of a transfer student.

4.2.6. Case Illustrations

The perspective of professionals involves a sample of suburban teachers who had classroom experience with city transfer students and were familiar with the students' academic and interpersonal adjustment to their new learning environments.

Teachers relate that a large proportion of transfer students were caught offguard by the higher expectations of their new teachers. This sometimes involved a protracted "recovery period" in remedial activities, but teachers are generally satisfied with student progress in this area. The experience of one suburban teacher belied the claim that only the brightest city students are transferring: "The range of students is from woefully unprepared to quite acceptable students." One teacher shared her empirical data of student achievement: "I kept the statistics this year for our school and I would say that probably 85 percent of the children improved at least slightly. Of the twenty-seven children, I would say that two of the girls were well above average and the rest were average. Nevertheless, all of the children improved by the end of the year. They are learning. Of course, we would rather have seen them come along a little quicker." A colleague from another district reported more substantial gains: "In testing the kids, I have found a tremendous growth in the two-year period. In fact, some have increased achievement scores as much as two and a half years."

These educators described a wide variance in the degree to which suburban districts are facilitating adjustment for teachers and students alike. Some districts are actively promoting teacher workshops on cultural diversity and fostering innovative approaches to teaching in a multiracial classroom setting. Other districts have been less motivated in this area, and teachers in these districts feel abandoned as a result. One teacher was unhappy with the "wait and see" attitude his central office had regarding the program: "The first year it was totally new for everybody; it was basically fumble around in the dark on your own and learn what you can through trial and error." Another teacher was suspicious of her district's motives: "I think a major problem and reason why many of us weren't well-prepared is because many of the districts (I know it's true for mine) were just dead-set against it right down to the wire. They thought they could weasel out of it because of the distance factor and avoid it with litigation; so they didn't waste any time or effort trying to make it work."

Also, there was a range of commitment among individual teachers: "Among members of our faculty there were teachers who said, "I'm not going to adjust my program'; and there were others who faced the fact that there had to be a period of growth and that teachers had to provide students airspace necessary for these kids to adjust."

Even in the districts that made an effort to help teachers prepare for this new experience, not all attempts were helpful: "I'm looking for something with more of a human dimension, human-to-human with different cultural backgrounds." Another said, "In my workshop I kept looking for the magic book with the answers because I didn't know anything. I needed someone to tell me how I could relate to black children on the same terms as I've always related to children in general. I think I could be more effective if I knew more; there's an awful lot I just don't know."

When asked to identify problems. transportation appears near the top of the teachers' list. They reported that the long bus ride affects the students and makes the transition from the bus to the classroom a sometimes problematic one. One related how late buses affected the student socialization process: "The children came in late and it separated the children even further. It set up a habit of being late; the city residents were embarrassed coming into the classrooms late; it was a bad problem." Regarding after-school activities, a teacher said, "We were disappointed to see the students hesitate to participate because they didn't want to get home too late." This is another liability associated with the long bus ride, according to this teacher.

63

Finally, teachers noted a heightened interest on the part of parents within the district. They are described as keeping a watchful eye on the desegregation process, especially the effect it has on the classroom dynamics, both academic and behavioral.

4.3. THE CENTRAL-OFFICE SCHOOL ADMINISTRATORS

Prior to the start of the focus groups in June, the project's director and research assistant met privately with all suburban school superintendents (or their representatives) in districts that are currently receiving city transfer students. What emerged from these meetings were several contrasting themes pertaining to the various school districts' approach to the process of voluntary interdistrict desegregation. The Associate Superintendent for Research and Evaluation and the Director of the Desegregation Monitoring Committee of the Saint Louis Public Schools were also consulted at this time.

The leaders of the Planning and Assessment Project interviewed the chief school officers or their representatives in sixteen of the school districts currently participating in the interdistrict transfer program. The purpose of these interviews was to determine the kinds of questions that ought to be asked of students and parents in the focus groups, to identify assets and liabilities of the first year of implementation from the perspective of high-level school administrators, and to identify what special staffing arrangements have been made to handle special circumstances associated with the interdistrict transfer program.

4.3.1. Support of Settlement Agreement

In general, the chief school officers supported the Settlement Agreement. Some were more enthusiastic than others about the benefits of multicultural education. But all supported the Agreement as the law and indicated that they planned to abide by it and do whatever they could to fulfill requirements.

4.3.2. Population-Specific Approaches for City and for Suburban Students

Although there was a common consent about the legality of requirements of the Settlement Agreement, there was much difference among school/district administrators about ways of handling transfer students. The suburban chief school officers were about equally divided among those who believed that special arrangements may

64

be necessary to accommodate city transfer students and those who believed that such students should be treated exactly like all others in a district. Those who believed that special assistance might be needed by some city transfer students tended to designate staff within central administration to provide or to coordinate the provision of such assistance.

School superintendents had grave concerns about the operation of transportation and said that transportation was a liability of the first year of implementation that threatened the future of the inter-district transfer program. Their criticisms were reported in our First Report of this program issued in October 1984. Corrective action has since been initiated by the state department of pupil transportation.

CHAPTER FIVE

COMMUNITY GROUPS

Representatives of twenty-six community groups were assembled to obtain the observations of their members on the voluntary interdistrict transfer desegregation program. Representatives from predominantly white groups were assembled in all-white focus groups, and some participated in integrated focus groups. Likewise, representatives of predominantly black groups were involved in all-black and in integrated focus groups. Groups that were represented in these situations can be categorized into the general classes of educational associations, neighborhood organizations, and civic or social-service agencies. Anonymity was promised to the participants.

Altogether, seven focus group sessions were held during the fall of 1984. The goal was similar to that of focus groups of students and parents. We wanted to obtain an assessment of the first year of the interdistrict school desegregation program from a variety of perspectives. The analysis presents the perspectives of individuals from predominantly white, predominantly black, and racially integrated community groups. These perspectives should not be interpreted as official policy positions of the organizations with which individuals were affiliated.

All community focus groups followed the same basic format. Participants were first asked to explain any connections, either formal or nonformal, between their organization and the city schools. The remainder of the discussion focused on identifying assets and limitations of the transfer program and steps that should be taken to improve it. Our analysis will indicate a series of ideas that may be classified as the black perspective and a series of ideas that may be classified as the white perspective. Points of convergence and divergence between the perspectives of representatives of these two racial populations will be identified. Their implications for community organization and action will be discussed.

66

5.1. BLACK COMMUNITY PERSPECTIVE ON THE TRANSFER PROGRAM

Most blacks active in local community groups believe that quality public education is essential for the future welfare of their race and for the vitality of the city. They see a vital and renewed municipality as beneficial to blacks because they doubt that whites will return to the central city in large numbers. They believe that current white residents of the city have given up on the public school.

The public school system has been permitted to deteriorate, local black community leaders believe, because the student body is predominantly black. Because of the pervasiveness of racism, most do not see a change in the public schools in the near future.

What to do about the city schools is the issue on which there is little consensus among black community leaders. Some advocate a return to neighborhood schools even if the student body of such schools is all black. Others have observed gross differences between city schools that serve predominantly black and predominantly white neighborhoods in Saint Louis. This realization has prompted them to question whether city schools that serve blacks will ever be brought up to par. Blacks are in accord, however, over the need for strong financial support in city schools and for renewed community involvement.

Some blacks are disparagingly characterized by fellow blacks as integrationists. Those who advocate racial integration in education usually support this approach because of personal experiences of integrated education in the past that were beneficial to them. Thus most blacks who support the policy of race mixing in public education tend to do so because of past positive experiences in integrated settings.

The black integrationists and the black separatists want similar educational outcomes: discipline in schools, low student-teacher ratios, adequate counseling, and expectations by teachers that black students can and do want to learn. The separatists do not believe that blacks will experience this kind of education in the suburbs because, they say, the teachers do not understand black culture and are not prepared to handle black children. The integrationists point out that whites have a stake in maintaining quality education in schools that their children as well as blacks attend.

67

Both integrationists and separatists were of the unanimous opinion that something must be done about the education of the poor blacks in the city. Solutions range from neighborhood control of schools, to the development of job-training programs for black teenagers, to the fostering of housing desegregation. Local black leaders are uncertain as to how much the local school bureaucracy wants help from community groups in solving this problem. Some thought well of the city school administration while others felt education decision makers had ignored or shoved aside community leaders.

Several black community leaders recognized that individual black students may have benefited from the interdistrict transfer program. However, their concern was for the black community and those children still enrolled in nonintegrated schools. They concluded that what helps black individuals does not always help the black community. Thus, they were critical of city black teachers and politicians who send their children to county schools.

Despite the range of differences in the black community on the school desegregation issue, the community leaders were together in support of public schools as the most appropriate setting within which to receive an education. They tended to oppose tuition tax credits for private schools as a threat to public education. It is fair to classify public education as a major source of hope among black community leaders in Saint Louis. Although black community leaders were critical of city public schools and often saw desegregation as a diffusion of black skill and power, they were almost unanimous in their appreciation of transfer as an option for individual students. Thus, while they support the voluntary interdistrict plan, they do not consider it a comprehensive solution to racial inequality in education for the Saint Louis area.

5.2. WHITE COMMUNITY PERSPECTIVES ON THE TRANSFER PROGRAM

White community leaders in Saint Louis are concerned about the reputation of the public schools. They report that many whites in the city have given up on public education and now send their children to private schools. These leaders believe that schools should play an important role in improving the image of Saint Louis, including its business climate. For this reason they agonize over what has happened to central-city schools for the liability they are for the city rather than the opportunity they should provide for the education of white children.

White community leaders, therefore, join with some blacks in declaring that desegregation has not worked. They bemoan the fact that funds are spent on transporting black children to suburban communities. They claim that such programs drain off the brightest and the best black students and further harm public education in the city.

The white community leaders do not hesitate to blame local education decision makers for the plight of Saint Louis schools. They give "chapter and verse" of instances in which they offered to help but were ignored by local school authorities. In summary, white community leaders say their interaction with the local school bureaucracy has been frustrating at best.

Some white community leaders are against the interdistrict transfer program not only because of its expense but also because they tend to believe that a serious gap exists between city students who are bused to the suburbs and local suburban students. They point to time spent on the bus as time that could be put to better use.

In general, white community leaders say that more money should be spent on Saint Louis schools, but they do not address the chronic inability of the system to raise revenue. The solution that most white community leaders advocate is housing desegregation. The neighborhood, they believe, is the place to begin integration, and this will lead to more meaningful school desegregation.

5.3. SIMILARITIES AND DIFFERENCES IN THE BLACK AND THE WHITE PERSPECTIVES

While white and black community leaders are similar in their perspectives that something is seriously and fundamentally wrong with the Saint Louis Public Schools, they have different reasons for seeking remedial action. Whites believe that good schools improve the image of the city, and blacks believe that a good education improves their race. While both groups wish for fundamental change, they despair of quick action because of racism.

Many black and white community leaders oppose the busing of city black children to suburban communities, apparently for different reasons. Some blacks are concerned that the best and brightest of their community are drained off at great harm to their racial community in the city. Whites are concerned about the expense to taxpayers of transporting city students to the suburbs. Also some whites assert the presence of a gap between city black students

69

and county white students; they wish to contain these alleged educational deficiencies within the city to protect their suburban racial community.

Black and white community leaders who support the voluntary interdistrict desegregation program probably do so for different reasons, too. Blacks apparently enroll their offspring in county districts for the educational benefits an individual may derive from schooling in such settings. Whole suburban systems tend to accept city blacks for the financial benefit a system may gain from participation in the interdistrict program.

Leaders, in both black and white communities, distrust the city school bureaucracy. Whites, however, have tended to give up on it more than blacks and have turned to private schools. Blacks identify quality public education as their great hope for the future. Thus, black community leaders are still willing to work with local school authorities and will give them the benefit of the doubt. They see limitations but continue to search for common causes and cooperative strategies. Blacks refuse to abandon public schooling in the city, although whites declare their faith is destroyed.

It is faith in desegregated education that is beginning to erode among some black community leaders. They believe that whites are uninterested in integration.

5.4. CASE ILLUSTRATIONS

Seven focus groups involving representatives of twenty-six local organizations were convened for the purpose of documenting the range of community opinion on the voluntary interdistrict transfer plan. The organizations represented a wide array of goals and objectives. Group discussions focused on the organization's official position on the settlement plan and a more general set of observations by participants on the assets and liabilities of the transfer program.

Black community leaders are deeply concerned by the striking disparity between the all-black North Saint Louis schools and the schools in South Saint Louis, and to an even greater extent, qualitative differences between city and county schools. One northside leader referred to his experience as a member of a research team that evaluated many of the city schools: "I have personally visited twenty-two of the schools with one of the field superintendents to look at the conditions of the schools. The conditions of the schools in the city

70

are so rank, some of those schools are over a hundred years old; the boiler plants, the windows, the electrical system are just decrepit. The result is a miserable learning atmosphere for the children enrolled in those schools." Another community representative related the problem of inequality in terms of a future dilemma. "Until something is done to improve city schools, you will be educating a class of children that still knows nothing about equality in education and will therefore not believe much about equality in opportunity." They attribute this to the legacy of a previously segregated system.

Relevant to this is a growing sense of mediocrity within the schools in North Saint Louis and this is viewed as a great danger to the future of the students and teachers involved in these schools. One woman with extensive experience in working with children who attend all-black Northside schools related, "These are good kids out there. They could benefit from the voluntary desegregation plan. What we have is a bankrupt system. We've got good kids with good minds that can be motivated but we lack even the materials to give them." She supported the interdistrict transfer program, but some members of the black community opposed it.

Representatives from a black group that staunchly opposes the plan contended, "We are made to feel ashamed because we want to be around our people. This plan is not about desegregation, it's about money. Real estate developers, bus companies, county school districts are getting rich off of deseg. funds." Added pressure is placed at the feet of teachers and counselors with the destabilization of the black family unit, claimed one black parent. There is also concern over the preparedness of suburban districts to address the needs of black children. One community leader questioned the capacity of suburban districts to cope with problems unique to transfer students: "Are the teachers given any workshops, training, or sensitivity? Are they made aware?"

An issue that dominates the discussion involving white community leaders of Greater Saint Louis is the desperate need for increased financial support of the city school system. Some see the transfer program a wasteful use of public monies: "I hate seeing this money being spent and it's not being spent on upgrading the schools. Why isn't the money being funnelled into the city schools?" Another added, "In order for the city schools to be viable, really viable, they have to address the issue of the education of kids in nonintegrated schools." Invariably they raise the question of whether funding set aside for the transfer program might not be better spent on upgrading

71

the city schools: "The biggest objection I have in addition to the denial of freedom of choices on the part of parents is the tremendous waste, as I see it, in time, effort, and money; it gives jobs to bus drivers, it also gives jobs to lawyers. As I see it, the only ones to have profited from this is the legal profession." In discussing alternative means of funding the schools, participants tended to overlook the obligation of the public to vote more funds for education at local and state levels of government.

Further attention is given to the public image of the school system and to its responsiveness to the local community. One leader from South Saint Louis illustrated the lack of confidence in the schools by referring to personal choices of local officials: "What percentage of the Board of Alderman of the City of Saint Louis who have children send them to the public schools? It's extremely low." These white leaders note the absence of a relationship between the Saint Louis Public Schools and the local businesses and neighborhood organizations. They report that the public schools are not used as a selling point to prospective buyers of neighborhood property. One redeveloper admits to having given up on the city public schools, saying, "Schooling is such a critical factor. We just quit marketing intentionally to families with children. We're not going to try and convince them that the schools are okay." He added some frustrations over the inconstancy of the relationship, adding, "At one time they (school leaders) called all the developers together and said 'We really want to work with developers', and then there was no follow-up. We spin our wheels a lot."

Though the discussion of issues appears to be distinguishable according to racial identity, there is also a wide sphere of interest upon which the perspectives converge. Of preeminent concern to members of black and of white community organizations is the need to improve the city schools, especially the sixty or so nonintegrated schools in North Saint Louis. One private-school official attributed the plight of the schools to a problem of community leverage: "If you want to apply a Darwinian model to schools, a survival of the fittest kind of notion, often schools deteriorate because the check and balance isn't there from somebody. The very people who would ordinarily stand up and say, 'Hey, wait a minute, this isn't right.' have either left the system or opted for magnet schools. So, the quality control ratio isn't there, the school does down." Another characterized the transfer opportunity as a double-edged sword, saying, "Yes, it does give those black children who have the opportunity to transfer to county schools another opportunity that may be

72

superior to the one they have at the school where they caught the bus, but it does very little to change that school they left."

There is some suspicion that the "best and brightest" youngsters are transferring to suburban districts at a disproportionate rate compared to peers from more academically and economically deprived backgrounds. Another representative from a private school system added, "I think it is a very satisfactory arrangement for the families who take advantage of it and who, in fact, are able to make a choice and be able to go to a school system that they perceive to be better. I think it is a total disaster for the city schools. They can say until they are blue in the face that it is not the best and brightest who are going; but they unquestionably are. All you have to do is talk to the teachers from the all-black Northside schools."

Related to the plight of the nonintegrated schools is a concern for the low morale of the teachers and local administrators in these schools. A private school central-office administrator offered, by way of comparison, its model of decentralized control at the schools: "We don't do anything from the central office except give them the kind of encouragement and support and resources they need from us. They're the ones on the line who will determine what will happen in those schools. The public school structure is such that it prevents local administrators from solving their own problems. Instead, they have to refer them upward and away from the school site." She added that one ramification of low faculty morale in the city is a "teacher migration" to the private and parochial schools: "We are getting what I would characterize as a large influx of applications from city public school teachers for positions in private schools. Their universal comment is that, 'We're tired, tired, tired, and I want to go somewhere we can teach.' And the extra three or four thousand dollars isn't worth the pain." At the same panel discussion a participant from one private system supported the notion of school-based management by saying, "Principals need to be empowered; they need to be able to have a say on staff selection and by God if they blow it, they ought to be nailed. Until that happens, until there's a sense that this thing's got to get better, nothing will happen."

Both racial groups also asserted the importance of strengthening the relationship between the neighborhood and the community. One black businessman viewed a strengthening of the city schools as one element in the revitalization of the total community: "The state has trouble understanding the vital link that exists between the schools and the job market. Strong, qualified graduates of public

73

schools translates, in most cases, into a more stabilized local community."

Finally, there is an appreciation for the smooth and peaceful implementation of the plan. This stands in stark contrast to the community violence experienced in other cities over the issue of school desegregation. A city official related that the profile of the desegregation issue is now on the wane: "I'd say the calls concerning public school desegregation and anything related to this have significantly decreased in the last year."

CHAPTER SIX

SUMMARY AND RECOMMENDATIONS

The Voluntary Interdistrict Transfer Program was approved by the court for the purpose of achieving constitutionally mandated unitary public school systems. The students who volunteer to participate in the program do so, according to their testimony and that of their parents, to achieve a better education. Thus, the success of a voluntary desegregation program depends upon the extent to which it fulfills the expectation of participants.

6.1. MAGNET SCHOOLS AS COMPREHENSIVE LEARNING ENVIRONMENTS

Magnet schools in the city that offer an extraordinary and specialized education have demonstrated that they can attract white suburban students. Magnet schools in Saint Louis are an important part of the Voluntary Interdistrict Transfer Program. The attendance of suburban white students in city magnet schools contributes to equity in the transfer arrangement, which otherwise would involve one-way busing of city students to the suburbs. To increase the enrollment of suburban students in Saint Louis magnet schools, these schools must be fully magnetized immediately. Magnet indicators that attract suburban white students are diversified student bodies, experienced and enthusiastic teachers, relatively small classes and the absence of overcrowding, a well-maintained physical plant, adequate instructional materials, and a variety of high-quality learning opportunities. The Saint Louis magnet schools have achieved some of these goals such as diversified student bodies, strong teaching staffs, and high-quality learning opportunities in special subjects. To retain their drawing power in the future, these schools must be fully magnetized. Physical plants should be renovated, appropriate levels of educational materials should be adequately provided, and the quality of learning opportunities should be upgraded in subjects that constitute the basic curriculum. Resources to achieve these ends should be made available immediately because of the unique and important function of magnet schools in the Voluntary Interdistrict Transfer Program.

6.2. MAGNET SCHOOLS AS DESEGREGATION TOOLS

Since magnet schools are for the purpose of achieving desegregation as well as enhancing education, the policy of restricting them to the city is a good one. The increasing enrollment of whites in these schools demonstrates that suburban residents will endure the hardship of traveling great distances for a quality education that fulfills a unique and special need. By limiting magnet schools to the city, suburban whites and city blacks are required to accept desegregation in their pursuit of a unique quality education. The practice of establishing magnet schools only within the city limits as part of the voluntary interdistrict desegregation program should be continued also as the most equitable way of achieving desegregation that evens up the transportation burden for both racial populations.

6.3. PLANNING NUMBER, KIND, AND LOCATION OF MAGNET SCHOOLS

Planning is urgently needed on (1) the optimum number of magnet schools that can serve the Saint Louis metropolitan area effectively, (2) the kinds of magnet schools that will achieve the two-fold goal of racial desegregation and enhanced education, and (3) the most appropriate location for magnet schools within the city. One gets the impression from testimony of educators, students, and parents that many decisions pertaining to these issues have been rendered on an ad hoc, uncoordinated basis. Because of the time and funding required to develop extraordinary learning environments, planning is essential to avoid arbitrary, capricious, and harmful public policies regarding the establishment of magnet schools.

6.4. SCREENING OF MAGNET-SCHOOL STUDENTS

The Saint Louis magnet schools have managed to accommodate students with a range of abilities. They are not reserved for the brightest and the best. While some teachers are critical of the range of students they must serve, we find the acceptance of all sorts and conditions of students to be a laudable practice for a public institution in a pluralistic society that strives to provide a universal education. Magnet schools should continue as unique and special schools, not elite and exclusive schools.

76

Some screening, of course, may be necessary to ensure that students who enroll in magnet schools have specific interests that correspond with the special focus of the school. Without such screening, magnet schools are used by some students to escape less interesting comprehensive regular schools. Students who transfer to magnet schools merely to avoid other less challenging schools are not as interested in the special courses of the magnet program and tend to impede the progress of others by their disinterest.

A number of screening methods for magnet schools are available, including tests of interests and evaluations by administrators and teachers. The screening method used should be one or a combination that is least discriminatory in terms of racial and cultural heritage. Moreover, the screening method used should identify special interests rather than ability. We recommend that the city magnet schools screen applicants and accept those whose interests correspond with the special focus of the school and at the same time continue to serve such students with a wide range of ability. To accomplish this, staffing, in terms of the experience of teachers, class size, and availability of educational materials in magnet schools should be comparable to those in the most reputable suburban school systems.

6.5. SCREENING OF CITY STUDENTS BY COUNTY SCHOOLS

Screening was discussed as an issue with reference to the acceptance of city blacks in suburban schools. Some city teachers and students charged that some suburban school systems were screening applicants and accepting only those with above average ability. However, suburban school systems have promptly denied any practice of rejecting transfer applicants except those students with a record of behavioral problems.

The interdistrict transfer program is primarily for the purpose of desegregating public schools; because of its voluntary nature, students tend to transfer to school districts they or their parents believe will enhance their education. Thus, suburban school systems are obligated to accept students who are within the upper and lower limits of the ability range of resident students. To avoid any suspicion of screening on the basis of ability, testing for the purpose of placing transfer students in appropriate academic programs should be permitted only after students have been accepted by a school district.

6.6. REFORMING THE TRANSPORTATION SYSTEM

Transportation is the life-blood of the interdistrict transfer program.

If it fails, the entire program fails. There was consensus among all that the transportation system during the first year of implementation had not worked properly. (For a full discussion of the transportation issue, see Chapter 1.)

6.7. APPOINTMENT OF PROGRAM COORDINATOR

Suburban school districts that receive city transfer students should assign responsibility to a specific administrator to oversee the operation of the interdistrict transfer program in that locality. School districts with a program coordinator tend to do a better job of integrating the newcomers into the system and sometimes solving problems before they occur. Conflicts involving students, teachers, and parents are handled by coordinators in a timely fashion and prevented them from blooming into major issues. A coordinator of the program is recognized by all participants as someone of authority to whom they can turn for assistance. Some school districts do not appoint program coordinators because they assert that the entire staff of central administration should be concerned about making the program work. Under this arrangement, typically no one is directly responsible for desegregation-related activities, thus inhibiting the development of a sense of continuity to the program. Reposing authority in the office of a coordinator for giving oversight to the interdistrict transfer program is essential to its effective intradistrict operation.

6.8. MORALE OF MAGNET-SCHOOL TEACHERS

Immediate attention should be given to ways of increasing the morale of Saint Louis magnet school teachers. Those with whom we talked appeared to be skilled teachers. Many had several years of professional experience. Beyond personal competence, however, there was an absence of excitement about their work, little spirit of teamwork, and no sense of community among professional colleagues. Indeed, there was a tendency by some teachers to put down others. It was reported that this behavior was largely the result of the rapid reassignment of teachers following their rehiring from layoffs in 1982.

Maybe experimentation with school-based management could be tried as one way of increasing the authority of local administrators and granting more autonomy to magnet schools to handle their own affairs. By increasing the sense of control over their destinies, the teachers who experience this may feel less victimized by a gigantic bureaucracy; they also may achieve a greater sense of community with professional colleagues associated with a particular magnet school.

6.9. HUMAN RELATIONS WORKSHOPS FOR STAFF

Human relations workshops and seminars in multicultural education are essential for all faculty in city magnet schools that receive county students, and for all faculty in county suburban schools that receive city students. The evidence is plentiful that teachers in these settings have made a range of adaptations to their new racially integrated classrooms, from total acceptance of transfer students to overt rejection. White teachers in the suburbs have ridiculed and stereotyped city transfer students as slow learners, and black teachers in city magnet schools have ridiculed and labeled county transfers as troubled students, behavior problems, and deviants who do not "fit in" with their suburban peers. Ridicule and rejection are extra burdens that transfer students who must adapt to a new learning environment do not need and should not have to bear.

Some school systems have provided opportunities for their professional staff to explore creative ways of handling classrooms of heterogeneous and diversified student populations. Others have not introduced such opportunities, believing that a "color-blind" approach is the best way to handle a desegregated student body. Where professionals are not alerted to the harm that may result from certain ways of interacting with students of groups that are different from their own, they often hurt students without realizing it. Even behavior that is intended to be helpful may in the end be harmful when teachers are unaware of the implications of their actions in a multicultural or interracial setting. The Voluntary Interdistrict Transfer Program is a deliberate way of achieving desegregation, and it should be accompanied by deliberate strategies that foster integration. Such strategies can be developed in workshops and seminars on human relations and multicultural education.

6.10 INVOLVEMENT OF PARENTS IN SCHOOLING

Despite the distance of their residence from school, our investigation has revealed an increased interest by parents of transfer students in their children's education. Whether such interest is translated into greater parental participation in school affairs depends largely upon individual teachers or schools and the frequency with which they communicate with parents about a child's progress or problem.

A policy study should be undertaken of effective ways that teachers and schools with transfer students have generated increased parental participation and whether these success experiences can be generalized to others. In this case, the concept of parental participation should not be limited to a parent's ability to appear at a schoolwide function. Rather, regular and candid parent-school communication, be it in person or by telephone, should be recognized as a key to building a productive home-school relationship.

Based upon the findings, both staffing and programs designed to increase parental involvement in schooling should be put in place for the next school year. Otherwise, parental participation in public education will continue to be limited largely to policy making as Board of Education members or to ad hoc and episodic arrangements. Systematic ways of involving representatives of all parents in the schools of transfer students are needed. The interest is there. But ways of tapping it and cultivating continuous parental involvement must be devised.

6.11. ORIENTATION

Our study has revealed that the adjustment of city students new to county schools or of county students new to city magnet schools is made easier by an orientation experience. Some school districts have instituted orientation programs; others have not. Our recommendation is that all schools that receive transfer students should have one or more orientation sessions specifically for the new students. The sessions may include a number of activities, including visits to the new campus by students and parents for the purpose of touring the facilities; informational meetings with teachers and administrators that explain the curriculum, schedule of classes, extracurricular activities, rules and regulations of the school; and introductions to local students who volunteer to serve as guides, companions, or "buddies" and to local households who volunteer to serve as host families. Whether elaborate or stripped down, orientation programs appear to be universally valuable and facilitate the introduction of students to their new learning environments.

6.12. SUMMARY

In summary, we recommend the following:

Magnet schools should be fully magnetized so that all courses, including special focus subjects and others, offer a high-quality education.

Magnet schools should be retained as demonstrated and effective ways of achieving racial desegregation in education. Adequate funding should be made available immediately for the purpose of renovating the physical plant, providing adequate instructional materials, and the enrichment of learning opportunities, including both basic and specialized curricula.

On-going planning is essential in determining the appropriate number, kind, and location of magnet schools that the Saint Louis metropolitan area should establish and maintain.

Magnet schools may screen applicants to determine whether their interests correspond with the special focus of the school, but they should accept students with a wide range of abilities, since their purpose is to provide a specialized and not an exclusive education.

Suburban schools are obligated to accept city students whose abilities are within the range of their resident students, and should require tests to assist in academic placement only after transfer students have been admitted to a school district, thus avoiding any suspicion of ability screening.

Transportation policy and practices, including the routing system, should be reviewed periodically and modified when circumstances warrant such attention. Careful scrutiny of student transportation will prevent a repetition of the frustrations of the first-year experience and, ultimately, lead to the successful long-term implementation of the settlement plan.

Coordinators should be appointed in all suburban school districts that receive city transfer students to give oversight to the inter-district desegregation program for the purpose of enhancing its effective operation.

Immediate attention should be given to ways of increasing the morale of magnet school teachers in those schools that are reported as experiencing serious problems related to morale.

Human relations workshops and seminars in multicultural education are necessary for teachers and other staff in city magnet schools that receive county students, and for faculty in county students that receive city students, to help them overcome the racist tendency to ridicule, stereotype, and falsely label students of racial and cultural groups that differ from their own.

A policy study should be undertaken of effective ways that teachers and schools with transfer students have generated increased parental participation and whether these successful experiences can be generalized to others.

The adjustment of city students new to county schools or of county students new to city magnet schools is made easier by an orientation experience that includes among other activities, visits to the new campus by students and parents, informational meetings, introduction of new students to "buddies" and host families. We strongly recommend that such support programs be introduced in school districts that do not currently sponsor them.

6.13. IMPLICATIONS FOR FURTHER STUDY

In our statement of the purposes and objectives of the Assessment and Planning project that was presented to the VICC, we stated that information collected should enable key educational policy makers to understand what happened during the first year of implementation; whether what happened is consistent with the intent of the plan; if so, how can we sustain the momentum; if not, what adjustments are necessary?

This project has focused largely on adjustments that are necessary to overcome problems identified in the assessment. Little has been said about the most successful ways "students have learned to cope with their new learning environments." This, then, is an area in need of further study.

A wonderful opportunity has been presented to the Saint Louis metropolitan area to discover how whites who volunteer to receive an education in a city magnet school setting and blacks who volunteer to receive an education in a county school cope in their new environments. These settings in which the black or the white students may be minorities are unusual and different from what they normally experience. They are settings without the normal support system to which these students have been accustomed. How do they persevere in these settings and overcome? What are the strengths of those who do this? What do they learn that they could not learn in a setting in which they are a majority? Much has been written about the value of the neighborhood school, but we know very little about the benefits that accrue to a stranger who is educated in a strange place. What does he or she give to and receive from such an experience? How does such an education compare to one that is received in more traditional surroundings?

In summary, we need to study such students who have made successful adaptations to their new and different learning environments so that we will have successful models to share with others. Further analysis is needed of black students in county schools who are successful and white students in city schools who are successful. These are areas of social science investigation that we tend to ignore.

Second, we need to study the students who are left out of the desegregation process. We need to study the adaptations of students in all-black schools in the city and the adaptations of students in the all-white schools in the county. We need to study these continuing models of segregation to determine what impact, if any, they have on the cognitive and affective learning of students and upon their individual and social goals. We need to compare and contrast these similar kinds of schools so far as desegregation is concerned to determine their strengths and weaknesses and whether they are similar or different from city and suburban schools that are no longer racially isolated.

CHAPTER SEVEN

CONCLUSIONS

7.1. THE EFFECTIVENESS OF THE INTERDISTRICT TRANSFER PROGRAM

In reviewing the most prominent issues identified by project participants, several important themes emerge as germane to all who were involved in the first year of the Voluntary Interdistrict Transfer Program. There is general agreement among Saint Louis educators and community leaders that the Voluntary Interdistrict Transfer Program is working well for participating students. Significant educational advantages are being gained by black city students transferring to suburban districts as well as for suburban students enrolled in city magnet schools.

However, many respondents expressed concern for black city students who remain enrolled in nonintegrated North Saint Louis schools. These schools are widely regarded as inadequate. Participants frequently noted the substantial disparity in the quality between these schools and others, including city magnet schools.

Another important inference drawn from the data is that participating districts must remain flexible in the procedures and strategies they use to address the needs of their transfer students. It is important to recognize that in subsequent years new transfer students may require a different level or a different type of attention than their predecessors. Districts must be prepared to modify their current transfer student policies if it becomes apparent that future students project needs different from those who preceded them.

Finally, an efficient transportation system is the most important feature of a viable interdistrict transfer program. A system that is unreliable leads to student and parent dissatisfaction and, in extreme cases, to withdrawal from the program. Considerable effort has recently been made by the State Transportation Office and the VICC to improve student transportation. Continuous monitoring of transportation will ensure the operation of an efficient system.

7.2. EDUCATIONAL THEORY AND PRACTICE

The transfer program would be well served by a serious effort by participating districts, both city and suburban, to acquaint teachers and students with the basic features of cultural, ethnic, and racial diversity. These activities received a strong endorsement from teachers who have participated in them; in turn, there is an urgent call for multicultural in-service training from teachers whose districts have not offered such programs. Teachers advise that the focus of these activities should be school or classroom-based, centered on such issues as cultural diversity, language differences, labeling, and the like.

The findings also indicate that, under certain conditions, suburban white students will transfer to integrated city magnet schools. The first criteron is that the magnet schools must provide curricular offerings that are indeed unique and specialized; the magnet school must offer something that cannot be received in the student's home suburban district. A second condition for transfer is a need for the level of instruction in the basic curriculum (nonspecialized subjects) to approximate the quality the students have grown accustomed to in county districts. A third condition is that the schools offer opportunities for wholesome interracial encounters.

Parental participation has been identified by suburban and magnet school teachers as a vital factor in the healthy academic and social adjustment of the students to their new schools. Teachers report that at first parents tend to be reluctant to approach the school to discuss their child's progress. However, once the school has initiated contact with the parent, a regular exchange sometimes follows. In fact, teacher-initiated communication, especially by a phone call, has often served to involve parents who have had a history of nonparticipation at other schools. The willingness of the school to initiate contact with parents seems to be associated with frequent parent-teacher communication, despite the geographical distance separating school and home.

Schools that have an identity of their own in which administrators and teachers feel in control of their destinies appear to have a higher level of morale among professionals and a greater sense of mission and community. Some schools in the city and suburban system have experimented with school-based management. The result of such projects should be documented and shared throughout the community.

7.3. RACE AND COMMUNITY RELATIONS

In understanding human action in a community setting, and particularly that which governs various forms of school desegregation and integration, it is necessary to use a method of analysis that considers complexes of characteristics rather than single traits.

Our study reveals that whites are attracted to city magnet schools because of the prospect of both high-quality education and integrated education; not one or the other, but both. It is this complex of characteristics that makes magnet schools attractive. Most of the whites who attend racially integrated magnet schools see diversity and high quality as linked or related experiences. It is probable that whites who seek this complex experience are attracted to it more than they are repelled from their existing schools.

Blacks, however, are probably repelled from segregated schools more than they are attracted to suburban schools. Blacks tend to leave segregated schools because of their past experience that such schools are deficient in one or more critical school-related variables.

The behavior of blacks and of whites who seek a desegregated education, therefore, can be understood only by way of analyzing a complex of characteristics; segregated schools and the quality of educational resources found therein as well as integrated schools and their quality of educational resources. Thus, the interest that some blacks manifest in desegregation is not a function of their desire to avoid members of their own race and to be with members of the dominant group. Rather, interest of some blacks in desegregated education is a function of their concern, on the one hand, for obtaining a better education and with their assessment, on the other, that such tends to be concentrated in a society where whites control the allocation of educational resources in predominantly white schools. Further, the desire by whites to attend an integrated school is not for the purpose of avoiding members of their own group. Rather, they realize that a comprehensive education involves both diversity and quality. Thus, a complex of characteristics is required to explain the behavior of both blacks and whites with reference to racial desegregation.

The relationship between race and socioeconomic status in education is a complex phenomenon that involves dominant and subdominant racial groups whose members occupy a variety of socioeconomic status positions. Within schools, there is cross-cultural contact among students of dissimilar socioeconomic status whose members are predominantly of one race, and cross-racial contact among students of dissimilar races whose members are similar in socioeconomic status. In the Saint Louis interdistrict desegregation program, for example, suburban white students, on average of a higher socioeconomic status than most of their peers in the receiving school, have transferred to some city institutions that are predominantly black; and city black students, on average of lower socioeconomic status than most of their peers in the receiving school, have transferred to some suburban institutions that are predominantly white. Since adaptation is a function of the situation and the characteristics of the people participating therein, group-specific solutions are necessary to accommodate both socioeconomic and racial variations in student populations. No single and simple solution is sufficient for race and socioeconomic-related experiences in education. Likewise, problems caused by race and racism cannot be properly addressed and corrected unless race is taken into account when fashioning a remedy. A "color-blind" approach in which all are treated in the same way is inappropriate, contraindicated, and, in extreme cases, may be unjust.

ABOUT THE AUTHORS

Charles V. Willie, a sociologist, is Professor of Education and Urban Studies, Graduate School of Education, Harvard University. He has served as a court-appointed master, expert witness, and educational planner in several school desegregation cases in such communities as Boston, Denver, Little Rock, and San Jose. A former president of the Eastern Sociological Society, he served by appointment of President Jimmy Carter on the President's Commission on Mental Health. Among recent books on education and desegregation are SCHOOL DESEGREGATION PLANS THAT WORK, COMMUNITY POLITICS AND EDUCATIONAL CHANGE, RACE, ETHNICITY AND SOCIOECONOMIC STATUS, THE IVORY AND EBONY TOWERS, and THE SOCIOLOGY OF URBAN EDUCATION.

Michael K. Grady, a candidate for the doctoral degree at the Graduate School of Education, Harvard University, is currently writing his dissertation on this analysis of the Saint Louis desegregation case. He has also served as an investigator and contributing author on research pertaining to desegregation finance, student dropout trends, college faculty development, and urban school improvement projects. He is presently living in Saint Louis and serving as research consultant to that city's Desegregation Monitoring and Advisory Committee.